NFC
5

50

Tom Petty & the Heartbreakers

GREATEST HITS

Book Editor: Tom Roed

Book Design: AWest and DZN

Photos by Dennis Callahan, Lynn Goldsmith, Robert Matheu, Neal Preston, Alison Reynolds, Steve Wilson.
Front and back cover photos by Dennis Callahan.

Correspondence with Tom Petty and the Heartbreakers
P.O. Box 260159, Encino, CA 91426-9998

"AMERICAN GIRL" (T. Petty); Producer: Denny Cordell (from TOM PETTY AND THE HEARTBREAKERS, 1976)

"Well it was kinda cold that night/
She stood alone on her balcony/
Yeah, she could hear the cars roll by/
Out on 441 like waves crashin' on the beach"

PETTY: "I remember writing the song about hearing the cars roll by because I was living in an apartment in Encino (CA) by the freeway. The sound was really annoying and we used to jokingly pretend it was the ocean. That's how that line worked itself in. I'm not sure exactly who the song is about—I think I just pictured a character for whom something had gone wrong. As a songwriter who was trying to write songs several years before this, I felt this one was a breakthrough for me—it gave me a theme—and I saw that I could write just a little bit wider than I had been...MIKE CAMPBELL and I were talking the other day about the recording session for the song. Nobody ever said anything about the Byrds or even thought about them. But even Roger McGuinn thought it was him when he heard the song and he quickly covered it. Musically, I wanted to do a beat like Bo Diddley. And the band's version of Bo Diddley turned into the beat you hear on this song."

"BREAKDOWN" (T. Petty); Producer: Denny Cordell (from TOM PETTY AND THE HEARTBREAKERS, 1976)

"It's alright if you love me/
It's alright if you don't/
I'm not afraid of you running away/
Honey, I get the feeling you won't"

PETTY: "It's a very cocky song, you know (laughs). I wrote it on the piano at the Shelter studio in Hollywood while the band was taking a break. When they came back, they heard it and said, 'Yeah, this is good, let's cut it.' And we did. It came in about seven minutes and at the end of the song MIKE played that lick. Everyone left and went home happy, but I stayed there playing with the tape. Then Dwight Twilley wandered into the studio as was typical back then when people were in and out all night. He heard the track and when it got to the end, he jumped up and said, 'Great lick, that's a great lick. You should move it up further. You're throwing it away.' At that point, it was two or three in the morning, but I called the band up at home and they came back to the studio. God knows what hour it was—we cut the song again with the new arrangement. I also want to mention the contribution of Phil Seymour, who recently died. On the next night, he happened into the studio and completely came up with that great arrangement for the background vocals. He said, 'Just give me two tracks and I'll show you this idea,' and I wound up getting more ideas. I'm sure that's why this song went over the top and is still a very good sounding record after all this time. Thanks, Phil."

"LISTEN TO HER HEART" (T. Petty); Producer: Denny Cordell, Noah Shark, Tom Petty (from YOU'RE GONNA GET IT, 1978)

***"You think you're gonna take her away/
With your money and your cocaine/
Keep thinkin' that her mind is gonna change/
But I know everything is okay/
She's gonna listen to her heart"***

PETTY: "While I was on the road, Jane (PETTY's wife) told me this story about how she went with our producer Denny Cordell to Ike Turner's house one night and was cornered by Ike in a scary circumstance. That is the little germ of an idea that started the song—we played it a lot onstage during our first tour before we even cut it—and I have Ike to thank for that. At the time, there was some controversy about the song. It was suggested that we change the word 'cocaine' to 'champagne.' That bothered me because it didn't mean the same thing at all. Cocaine is much more expensive than champagne and it didn't put it in the proper light for me. I thought since the song was putting the drug in a very negative context, there shouldn't have been anything wrong with it, but I do think that some stations wouldn't play it because of that."

"I NEED TO KNOW" (T. Petty); Producer: Denny Cordell, Noah Shark, Tom Petty (from YOU'RE GONNA GET IT, 1978)

"All of a sudden it's me on the outside"

PETTY: "Alienation! (laughs). Looking back, my thoughts from this period were very blunt, just little bursts of adrenalin. At the time, we were getting described as 'urgent.' I must have felt that way. But to me it wasn't obvious. You don't write the song and say, 'That's urgent.' We just wanted to make rock & roll records and ones that didn't embarrass us. The song was actually inspired by Wilson Pickett's 'Land of a Thousand Dances.' It's almost the same riff, but with a different beat. I wanted a track like Wilson Pickett. Of course, it came out sounding nothing like Wilson Pickett, but it's a pretty good song."

"REFUGEE" (T. Petty, M. Campbell); Producer: Tom Petty, Jimmy Iovine (from DAMN THE TORPEDOES, 1979)

***"It don't really matter to me, baby/
Everybody's had to fight to be free"***

PETTY: "Yeah, it was a real put-down. It was like, 'Don't bother me, I've got my own problems.' Sometimes it's hard for me to sing it now, because I'm not that mad. It's an angry, sarcastic song. I'm surprised it was as popular as it was...All I can really remember about writing it is that it didn't take very long. MIKE gave me a tape of some music he had recorded on his multi-track recorder at home. I kept it and later put it on and walked around my room. In what seems like ten or fifteen minutes, the song burst out. I played it to MIKE and he got visibly excited, crazy. I also remember when I met Jimmy Iovine (the producer) in the studio and played him the song. He just started hittin' his head, you know, with his palm and walking around going, 'Wow, wow, wow!' That was the easy part. But making the record was probably the toughest thing we ever had to do in the studio. We couldn't seem to get it to the point where we liked it. We kept coming back to it during the recording of the album. I think we did over 100 takes before we finally landed the one that made it on the album."

"DON'T DO ME LIKE THAT" (T. Petty); Producer: Tom Petty, Jimmy Iovine (from DAMN THE TORPEDOES, 1979)

***"Someday I might need you, baby/
Don't do me like that"***

PETTY: "Jimmy (Iovine) is a thorough type of guy. He went through all my old songs and suggested we record this one from the Mudcrutch album (PETTY's early band which included future HEARTBREAKERS' MIKE CAMPBELL and BENMONT TENCH). Initially, we didn't want to do it because we wanted no ties to the past. But we cut it in one night: we recorded a few takes, played it back a couple of times, then put it away. When the album was finished, our assistant engineer said, 'I really hate to speak up, but you should get this tape out and do it again.' We thought it sounded pretty good and it turned out to be the first hit of the album. It's based on something my dad used to say, 'Don't do me like that.' My father never asked for royalties, but he was pleased that I used his saying. He has given me about a dozen since, but none of them are as good."

"EVEN THE LOSERS" (T. Petty); Producer: Tom Petty, Jimmy Iovine (from DAMN THE TORPEDOES, 1979)

***"Baby, even the losers get lucky sometimes/
Even the losers keep a little bit of pride"***

PETTY: "I think it means something to people, you know. I think it's a very good line. I was very pleased when I came up with the chorus, especially because when I went into the studio I didn't have it. I really didn't. I had all of the song except the chorus. I had the chorus music, I had the melody, but I didn't know what words would fit there. It was the strangest thing—we were rehearsing it on the floor of the studio and it just came out of me. I think in a way the line to the song is so much about me and it always had the feel that maybe it's about the last years I was in Florida before I came here. But the title made it much more of an anthem that so many people could identify with for different reasons. It's great when you can write something that uplifts people as long as you're not doing it in a deliberate fashion or like a greeting card. The song was never released as a single, but it was on the radio a lot. At every show, they yell for it."

"HERE COMES MY GIRL" (T. Petty, M. Campbell); Producer: Tom Petty, Jimmy Iovine (from DAMN THE TORPEDOES, 1979)

> ***"You know sometimes I don't know why/***
> ***But this old town seems so hopeless/***
> ***I ain't really sure, but it seems I remember/***
> ***The good times were just a little bit more in focus"***

PETTY: "During this time, we were under lots of pressure. People were suing us for all kinds of stuff. I guess the song is about taking comfort where you can find it—life's tough, but here comes my girl. People tell me it's kind of become a popular wedding song—I'm happy it's found its place...The narration in the song was inspired by stuff we heard Blondie do when we toured with them, the chorus is definitely inspired by the Byrds, and the drum beat is pretty identical to 'Walk This Way' by Aerosmith...we thought that it was a great beat."

"THE WAITING" (T. Petty); Producer: Tom Petty, Jimmy Iovine (from HARD PROMISES, 1981)

> ***"You take it on faith, you take it to the heart/***
> ***The waiting is the hardest part"***

PETTY: "I have to thank Roger McGuinn for inspiring me with that line. Back in 1978, I went out to a club in Huntington Beach to see the Byrds with McGuinn, David Crosby and Gene Clark. From my conversation with Roger backstage—he would later remind me of this—I actually took two different images. There was one about how he was living in Century City at the time, which to me was just mind-boggling because I hated Century City. I was being sued at the time and I had to go there all the time. I just thought 'it's this corporate-awful place.' That inspired one song ("Century City"). And Roger also said to me something about—I don't know what context it came up in—the waiting is the hardest part. And I thought, 'whoa, what a line!' It's a really good line and very true. I mean, I knew what it was like to be at gigs where you'd be there just milling around all afternoon and the hardest part of all is just waiting to get on. For the song, I just tried to get it in one general context...Before we recorded the album, I remember I had gotten my new Rickenbacker twelve-string that was much better than the one I had before. It's featured prominently on the album. And Mike played some very good stuff on it...This is not my favorite single, as far as the performance style goes. We probably couldn've played it better than we did. Though it's not bad, we did the job, but I think the song is better than the record."

"YOU GOT LUCKY" (T. Petty, M. Campbell); Producer: Tom Petty, Jimmy Iovine (from LONG AFTER DARK, 1982)

> ***"You got lucky babe, when I found you"***

PETTY: "The sheer gall of the song—its sarcasm—is unforgivable (laughs)! I wrote it in a way that you couldn't possibly believe the sentiment of the person singing it. You could see they were actually hurt so badly that they were reacting in an extremely ridiculous way. It was a last gasp defense...I got the idea for it from a song from Elvis' Kid Galahad movie called 'I Got Lucky.' I always thought it was such a dumb song and it would be really funny to turn it around and sing, 'You got lucky when I found you.'...This was the first song on which BENMONT (TENCH) ever used a synth. Honestly, this album was the first time I started to feel a little restless musically. I thought we were doing something good, but we weren't really doing anything we hadn't done before. I think bringing the synth in was part of just trying to shock us into moving on because you have to be careful you don't make the same records again and again. I felt like we had to try to find some other turf."

"DON'T COME AROUND HERE NO MORE" (T. Petty, David A. Stewart); Producer: Tom Petty, David A. Stewart, Jimmy Iovine (from SOUTHERN ACCENTS, 1985)

> ***"Whatever you're looking for/***
> ***Hey, don't come around here no more"***

PETTY: "When I heard it on the playback of this greatest hits album, I was really moved by it because it was from a very down point in my life. It's funny how you write something when you don't necessarily think it's about you and then maybe ten years later when you hear it, you're positive it was about you. I was going through a rough time in my personal life and this song is so spooky. Dave Stewart and I worked on the single for a solid straight month and it was a big job with lots of people involved: girl singers, a cello player, and other stuff. The HEARTBREAKERS were horrified at first. They just thought that I had lost my mind. It was a very unusual single, but I think it's one of my top two favorite singles we ever made. By this point, the musical chains were off and Dave was a big part of that. Music was changing again, and the Eurythmics were part of this whole other onslaught of British bands. Very few of them were good, but I thought—and still feel this way—Dave was just an incredibly talented songwriter. I made a point to actually seek him out. And we had such a wild time doing the song at my house. We had a cello player come over who had never played without musical charts. When he got to the house, he said to Dave and I, 'Where's the music?' He also came on a day when Dave and I had been to Nudie's. We had on cowboy hats and boots, and in walks this guy from the L.A. Philharmonic asking for charts and we said, 'Well, we don't really have any music.' He said, 'Well, I've never played without music.' At this point, Dave says, 'Burt, you're gonna have a good time tonight.' We told this guy to just play whatever came to his mind and by the end of the night, Burt was wearing a cowboy hat and having a great time."

"I WON'T BACK DOWN" (T. Petty, Jeff Lynne); Producer: Jeff Lynne, Tom Petty, Mike Campbell (from FULL MOON FEVER, 1989)

> ***"You can stand me up at the gates of hell/***
> ***But I won't back down"***

PETTY: "I think this was probably inspired by the fire—when my house was burned down by an arsonist. I was at a point in my life where I was just really getting my shit together, as they say, and then this happened. It was a very traumatic experience to just lose everything. The only choice I had was to make it through and be as stubborn as this song is. That was probably my subconscious thought behind writing it. It's interesting—I get a lot of letters from people who'll tell me how I helped them through a crisis with this song. I'm most proud of it for that reason. And I was very moved when I heard about the pro-choice doctor who was recently killed. Before his death, he had been at a rally, standing up on his car playing the song —he adopted it as his theme because he was being harassed—through the car speakers. He was soon murdered and then they played this song for him at a gathering...This is probably my favorite single I was ever involved in. It's rare that you can get on tape everything the way you pictured it in your mind. The single sounded exactly like I thought it should, though I had a lot of help from a lot of really good people."

"RUNNIN' DOWN A DREAM" (T. Petty, J. Lynne, M. Campbell); Producer: Jeff Lynne, Tom Petty, Mike Campbell (from FULL MOON FEVER, 1989)

"There's something good waitin' down this road/ I'm pickin' up whatever's mine"

PETTY: "I think FULL MOON FEVER in general caught me in a very optimistic and hopeful mood. It didn't feel like I had to be serious. I just wanted to amuse myself and have some fun. It was great working with Jeff Lynne, the most talented musician I ever met and an incredible producer, very underrated in the grand scheme of things. I have to give him credit for helping me because everything was realized so quickly that it made recording the album twice as much fun. There was no 'work' involved or headaches with the LP. Nothing was difficult—it was all recorded in a garage and a bedroom. The song also has one of the last great guitar riffs. I think it's a priceless riff by MIKE and I wanted to write a song around it. I kept thinking this should be a driving kind of song. Truthfully, I don't think I've ever written too many songs about cars or driving, but I got into the idea and I also have a little verse in there for Del Shannon. I pictured the character in the song singing in his car to 'Runaway,' (Shannon's classic hit) which sort of also set the tone of escaping and running away; Del's hit was probably one of the first great 'I'm running away from it all' kind of songs. Del was going through a little bit of a down period and I thought it would cheer him up. So I put that in there and the rest of the song came pretty easily after that. I heard it on the radio recently. It sounded pretty good. At the end, the DJ said this song would be one of the major defenses in favor of speeding. It does make you want to drive real fast."

"FREE FALLIN'" (T. Petty, J. Lynne); Producer: Jeff Lynne, Tom Petty, Mike Campbell (from FULL MOON FEVER, 1989)

"I wanna free fall out into nothin'/ Gonna leave this world for awhile"

PETTY: "This was written stream-of-consciousness in minutes, maybe the quickest song I ever wrote. I think I was writing the entire lyric to amuse Jeff—whose great contribution was the title—because he was sitting at my side. I would sing, 'She's a good girl, loves her mama,' just trying to make him smile and he kept nodding for me to keep going—he had a cassette running and that was it. The next day, we barreled over to MIKE's house where we laid the song down right away. That was where I made my decision to make a solo album because I didn't want to call in the band to recut the song. I was too pleased with what I had done and I was enjoying the freedom of no politics in the studio. It was a refreshing change."

"LEARNING TO FLY" (T. Petty, J. Lynne); Producer: Jeff Lynne, Tom Petty, Mike Campbell

(from INTO THE GREAT WIDE OPEN, 1991)

"Well the good 'ol days, may not return/ And the rocks might melt and the sea may burn/ I'm learning to fly/ But I ain't got wings"

PETTY: "I really loved that song and still do. I think I was coming to grips with the view that you can be optimistic, hopeful and as good a person as you want to be, but it's not going to make life simple for you. Nothing will. You can have all the success you want and it's not going to make your life—really your personal life—much easier than anyone else's. The song was also influenced by the Gulf War. It was written during the time the war was breaking out, everything was very grey, and there were burning oceans and oil fires. I was disappointed by the war and the attitude of the American people. I certainly didn't blame the soldiers for going there, but I felt that few people wanted to challenge the Bush administration on its lies. It was a bad time and I really think it influenced the whole tone of the album."

"INTO THE GREAT WIDE OPEN" (T. Petty, J. Lynne); Producer: Jeff Lynne, Tom Petty, Mike Campbell

(from INTO THE GREAT WIDE OPEN, 1991)

"His leather jacket had chains that would jingle/ They both met movie stars, partied and mingled"

PETTY: "Yeah, I was stretching it a bit there (laughs), but it was just so funny when I thought of the rhyme, I had to use it. The song is a classic music business story and a comment on how these days, artists—especially new artists—are so much at the mercy of this big business deal where if you suddenly don't come up with something like your last one or whatever, you're just immediately out of the game and they'll bring somebody else in who can play ball. The song was just a little story—almost like a screenplay, really—and I tried to write it cinematically. When the video was shot in Hollywood, it was very hard to tell where the set ended—the line was blurred between the extras and the real people on the streets."

"MARY JANE'S LAST DANCE" (T. Petty); Producer: Rick Rubin, Tom Petty, Mike Campbell (from GREATEST HITS, 1993)

"There's pigeons down on Market Square/ She's standing in her underwear/ Lookin' down from a hotel room/ Nightfall will be coming soon"

PETTY: "I'm still trying to figure out exactly what this song is about. I think it's kind of at the end of something; it's about someone whose little world is gone and they're trying to make the best of it. I'm not sure what it means and it will be some time before I identify it...For this, we put away the acoustic guitars that FULL MOON FEVER and INTO THE GREAT WIDE OPEN were based on. I was very hung up on acoustic guitars and the textures they could create. But I thought I better challenge myself a bit and do a record without Jeff Lynne because I'll start to lean on him. It was certainly no reflection on him because he's one of my favorite people. So MIKE suggested Rick Rubin, whom he had just met. I think he was impressed with Rick's instincts and enthusiasm. And that was really what we needed: someone who just keeps us enthused about what we're doing, because the HEARTBREAKERS themselves know each other so well that it's easy for us to get discouraged or depressed. We're also the five most impatient people I've ever met and we get bored so fast that we should probably seek therapy. We thought we should go into the studio and perform the songs live, something we haven't done in a long time. Jeff Lynne's recording approach is like that of a painter: there are a lot of overdubs and each color is added very carefully. Rick comes from the filmic approach. It's like he says, 'I'm going to roll the camera, light it just right and we're gonna grab it.' I knew that would inspire the band. We went in to cut two songs and wound up playing as many as 30 new ones in the session."

"SOMETHING IN THE AIR" (John Keene); Producer: Rick Rubin, Tom Petty, Mike Campbell (from GREATEST HITS, 1993)

"Call out the instigator/ Because there's something in the air/ We got to get it together sooner or later/ Because the revolution's here"

PETTY: "We played this Thunderclap Newman song from 1969 on the road a couple of tours back. We all loved the song. I was afraid that it wouldn't make its way onto an album because we've always been so hard on covers—they just never seem to get priority over the original material. I thought this would be a good opportunity to put this on an album. I think it's a good song and it's still timely today. When we recorded it, we purposely didn't listen to the original version—we didn't want to be too exposed to it. Also, this is the first time that HOWIE (EPSTEIN) and I sang lead together through the whole song...Yeah, I think we still need to keep calling out the instigators."

AMERICAN GIRL

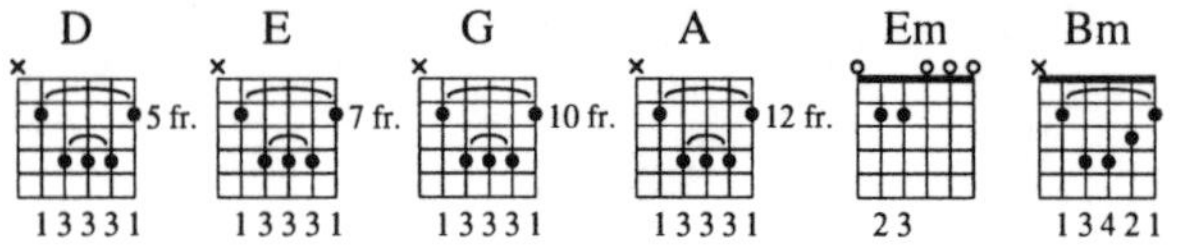

Words and Music by
TOM PETTY

Bright rock ♩ = 244

w/Rhy. Fig. 1

E
G
A
1. 2.
3.
Ooh.
(end Rhy. Fig. 1b)
Verses 1 & 2:
w/Rhy. Figs. 1, 1a, & 1b
D
E
1. Well she was an A - mer - i - can girl,
2. See additional lyrics.
G
A
raised on prom - is - es.
hold
T
A
B

D
E
She could - n't help think - ing that there was a
G
A
lit - tle more to life some - where else.
hold
hold
D
Af - ter all it was a great big world,
G
Em
with lots of plac - es to run to.

A
Yeah, and if she had to die, try - in' she
hold
had one lit - tle prom - ise she was gon - na keep.
Chorus:
G
A
Oh, yeah, al - right
hold
D
Bm
take it eas - y ba - by, make it last all night.

G
A
She was an A - mer - i - can
w/Rhy. Figs. 1, 1a & 1b
D
girl.
1.
2.
N.C.
1.2.3.
4.
w/Rhy. Figs. 1, 1a & 1b
D
E
G
A
Play 3 times.

Verse 2:
Well it was kinda cold that night,
She stood alone on a balcony.
Yeah, she could hear the cars roll by
Out on 441, like waves crashin' on the beach.

And for one desperate moment there
He crept back in her memory.
God, it's so painful,
Something that's so close
But still so far out of reach.
(To Chorus:)

BREAKDOWN

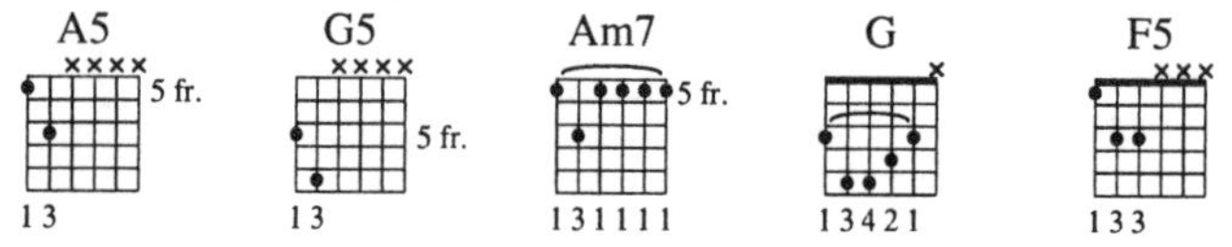

Words and Music by
TOM PETTY

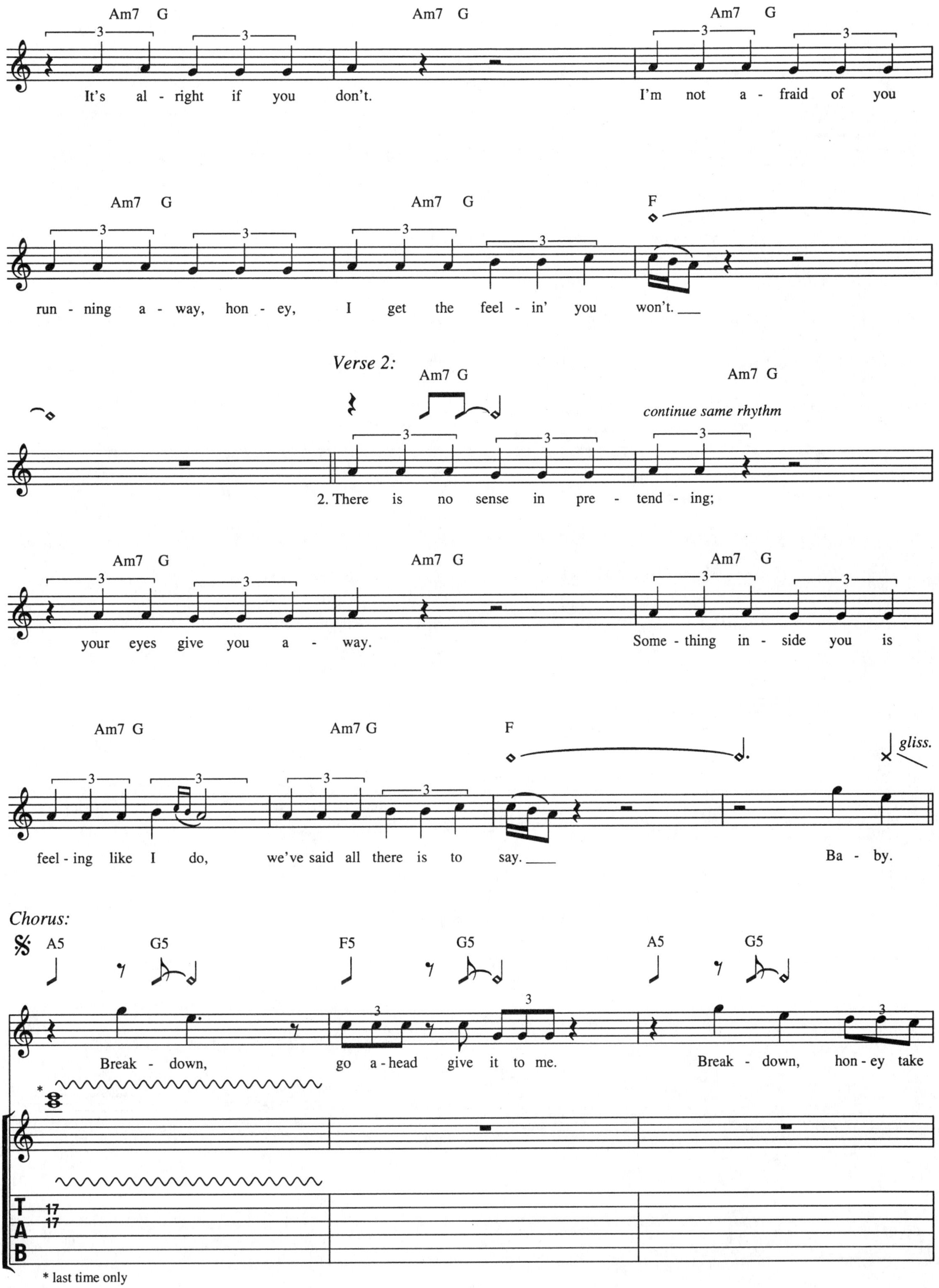
Am7 G Am7 G Am7 G
It's al - right if you don't. I'm not a - fraid of you
Am7 G Am7 G F
run - ning a - way, hon - ey, I get the feel - in' you won't.
Verse 2:
Am7 G Am7 G
continue same rhythm
2. There is no sense in pre - tend - ing;
Am7 G Am7 G Am7 G
your eyes give you a - way. Some - thing in - side you is
Am7 G Am7 G F
gliss.
feel - ing like I do, we've said all there is to say. Ba - by.
Chorus:
A5 G5 F5 G5 A5 G5
Break - down, go a - head give it to me. Break - down, hon - ey take
T
A
B
* last time only

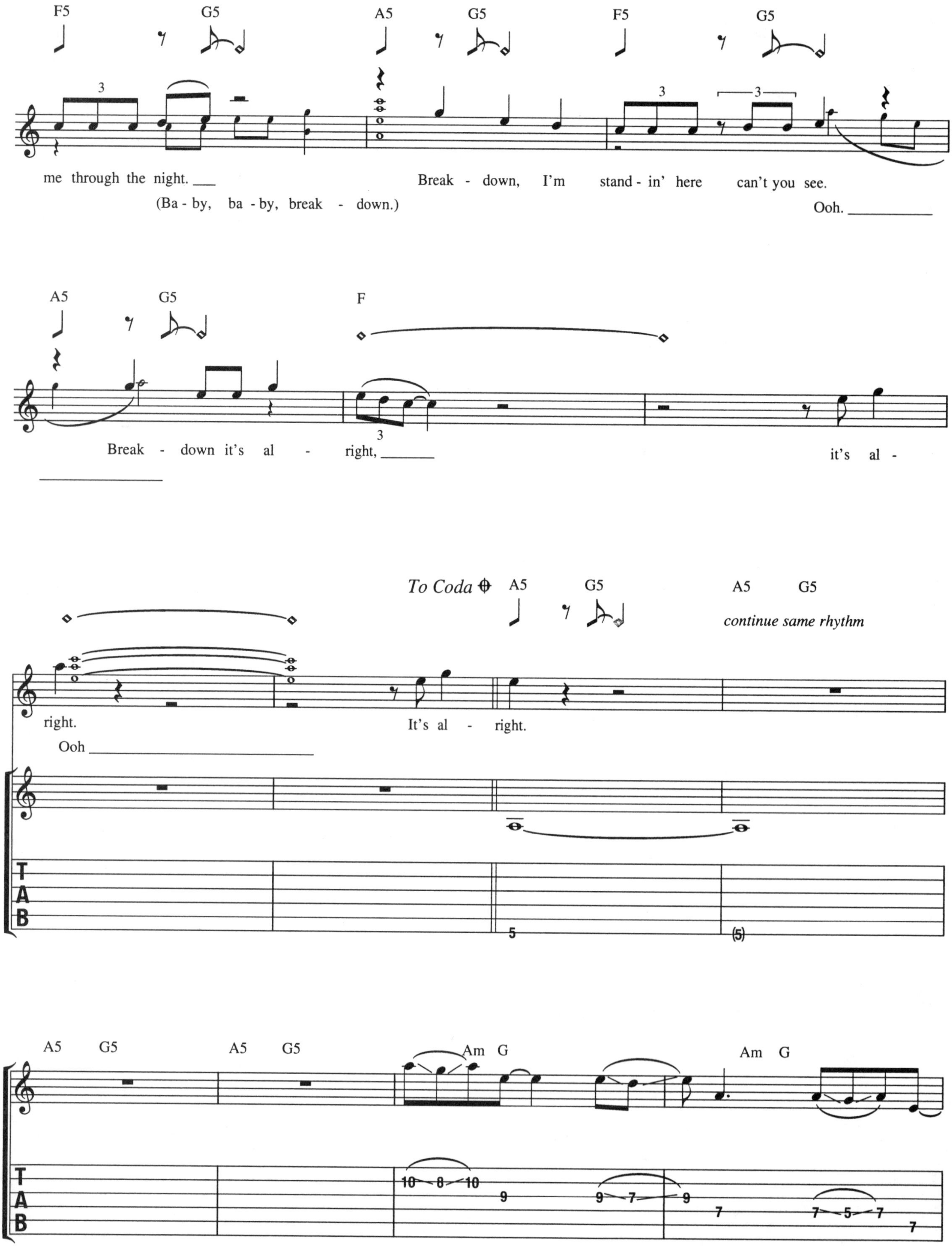
F5 G5 A5 G5 F5 G5
me through the night.
(Ba - by, ba - by, break - down.)
Break - down, I'm stand - in' here can't you see.
Ooh.
A5 G5 F
Break - down it's al - right,
it's al -
To Coda
A5 G5 A5 G5
continue same rhythm
right.
Ooh
It's al - right.
A5 G5 A5 G5 Am G Am G

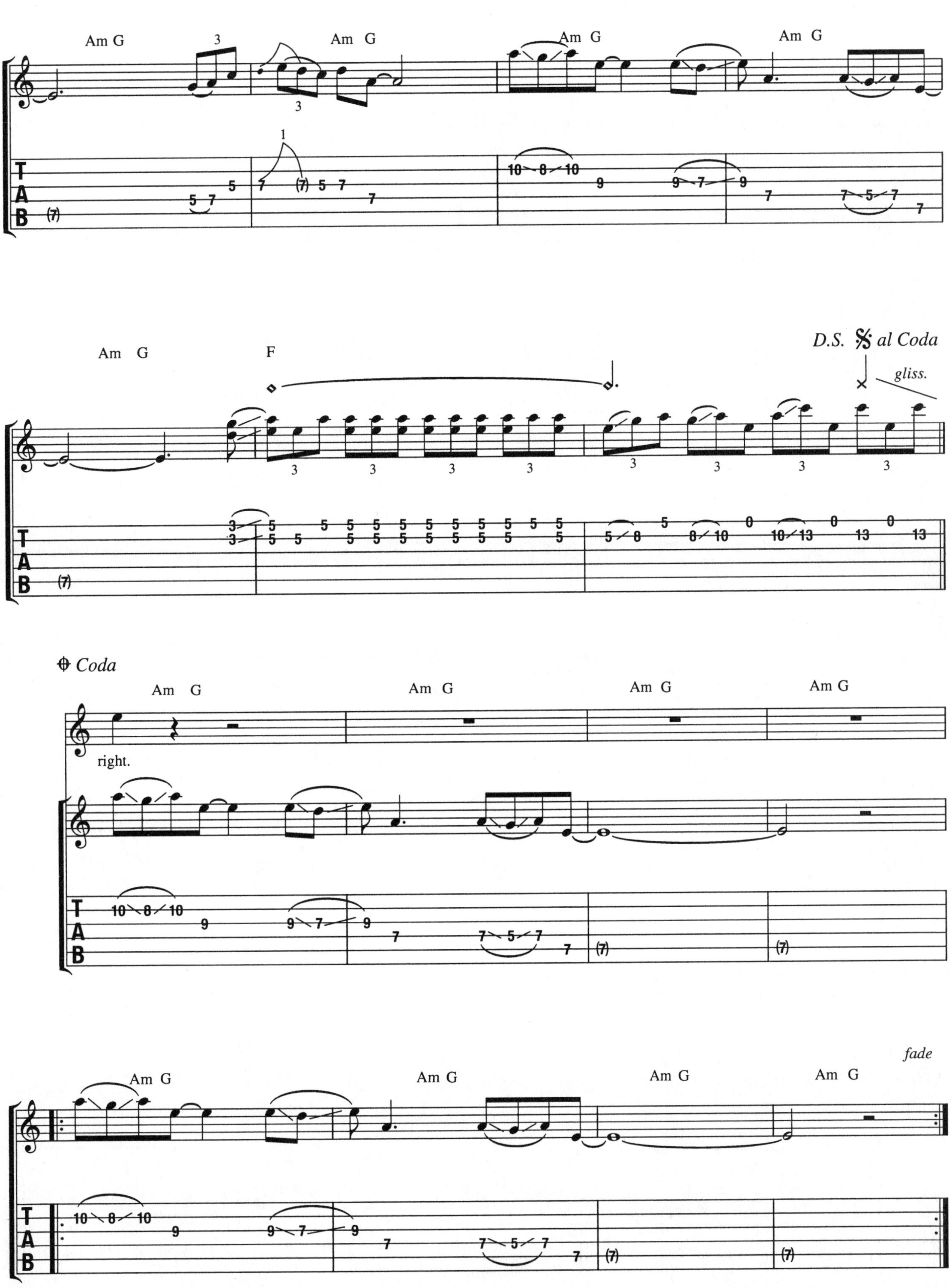
Am G
Am G
Am G
Am G
Am G
F
D.S. al Coda
gliss.
Coda
Am G
Am G
Am G
Am G
right.
fade
Am G
Am G
Am G
Am G

LISTEN TO HER HEART

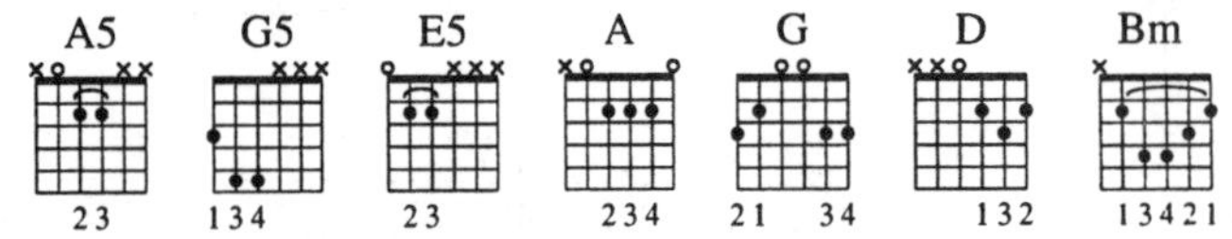

Words and Music by
TOM PETTY

P.M.
mind is gon - na change, _ but I know ev - 'ry - thing is o - kay. She's gon - na
Chorus: G5 A5
Gtr. 2
(simile rhythm)
listen to her heart. ___ It's gon- na tell her what to
Gtr. 1
Rhy. Fig. 3
(end Rhy. Fig. 3)
Let ring
To Coda
A5 E5
do. She might need a lot of lov - in' but she don't need __
1.
A
w/Rhy. Figs. 1 & 2 (1st 2 bars only)
you.
2.
A5 w/Rhy. Fig. 3
you.

Bridge:
G
A
Gtr. 1
And you just can't creep up be - hind her.
Gtr. 2
harm.
8va
(8va)
And you can't un- der- stand ___ that she's
A
E5
P.M.
my girl. She's my __ girl. ___
Yeah!
Solo: w/Rhy. Fig. 2 (2 times)
w/Rhy. Riff 1 (4 times)
A5
Rhy. Riff 1
Gtr. 1
Let ring

Verse 2:
You want me to think that I'm being used,
You want her to think it's over.
You can't see it doesn't matter what you do,
An' buddy you don't even know her.
(To Chorus:)

I NEED TO KNOW

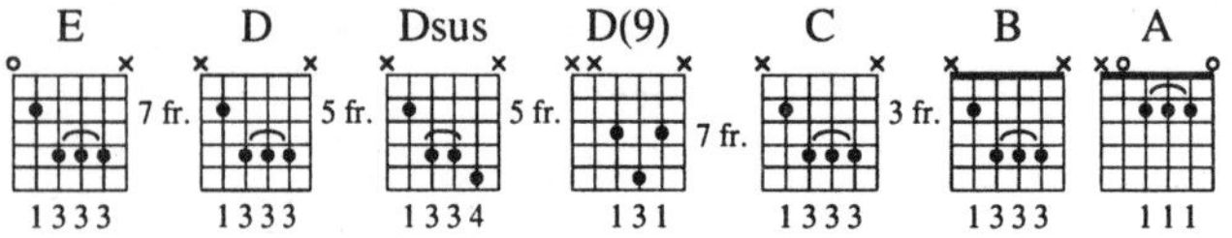

Moderate rock ♩ = 152

Words and Music by
TOM PETTY

Chorus:
E D E D(9) E
I need to know, I need to
(I need to know,)
hold
T A B
D C D
know if you think you're gon - na leave then you bet - ter say so. I need to
(I need to know.)
(hold)
E D C
know, I need to know be - cause I don't know how long
(I need to know,) (I need to know.)
(hold)
D C
I can hold on. If you're mak - in' me wait,
D
if you're lead - ing me on, I need to

last time w/Rhy. Fig.1 (3 times)
To Coda
E D E D(9) D E D E
know, __
(I need to know.)
I need to know.
(I need to know.)
1. D(9) D
2. D(9) D
Guitar Solo:
A
E
A
Rhy. Fig. 1
E D
E D

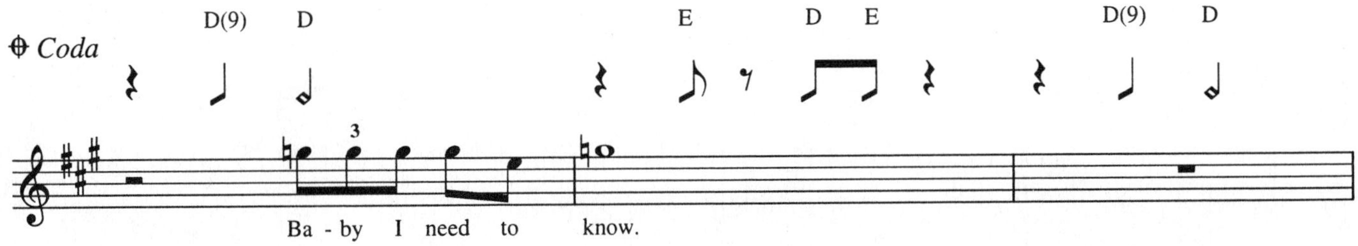

Verse 2:
Who would have thought that you'd fall for his line.
All of a sudden it's me on the outside.
(To Chorus:)

REFUGEE

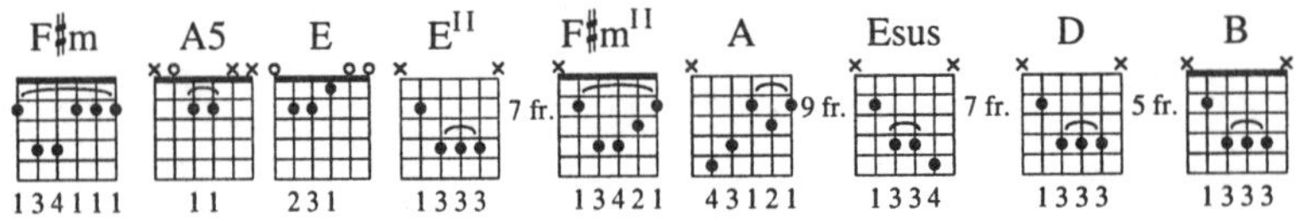

Moderate rock ♩ = 116

Intro:

Words and Music by
TOM PETTY and MIKE CAMPBELL

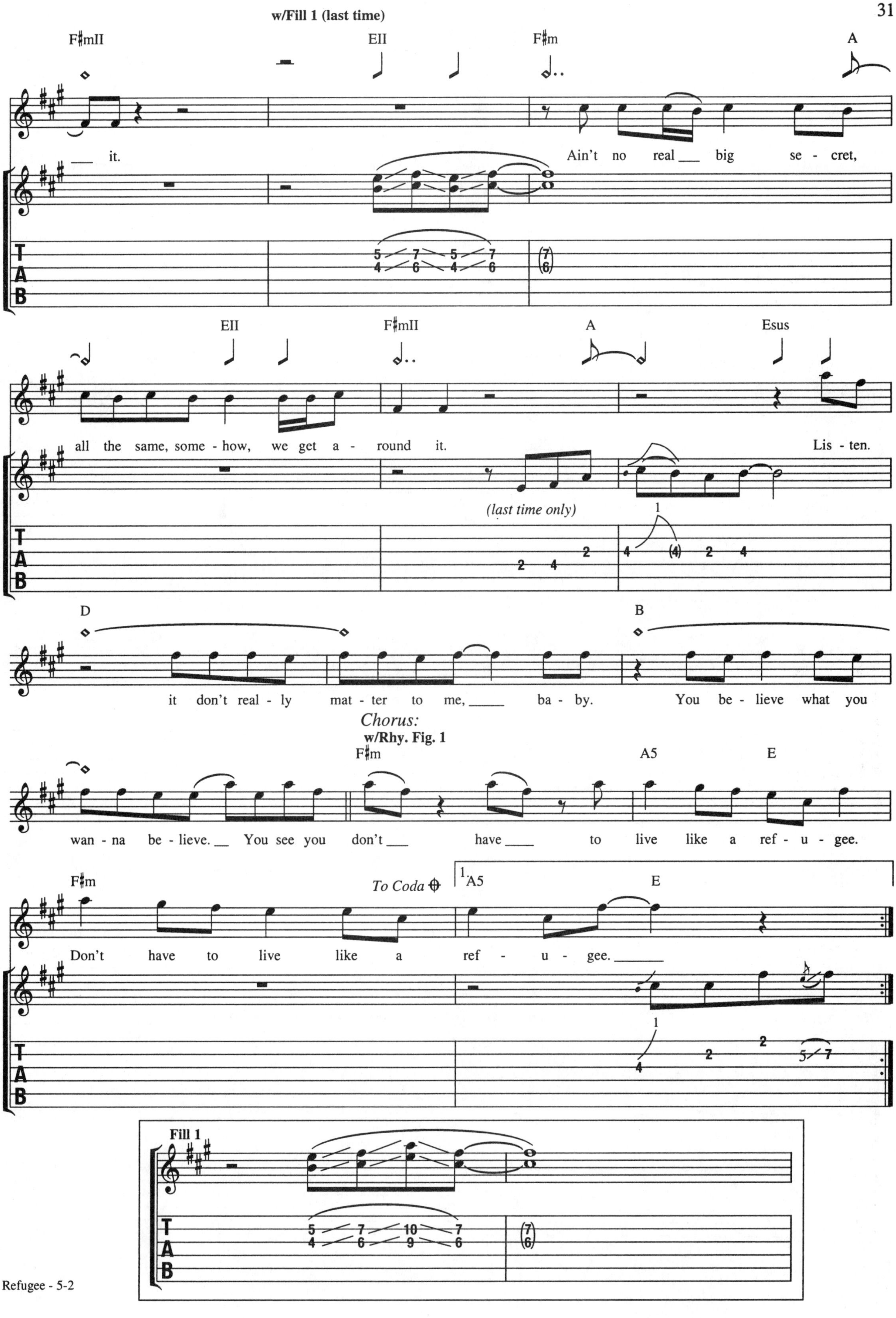
w/Fill 1 (last time)
F♯mII
EII
F♯m
A
it.
Ain't no real big se - cret,
EII
F♯mII
A
Esus
all the same, some - how, we get a - round it.
Lis - ten.
(last time only)
D
B
it don't real - ly mat - ter to me, ba - by.
You be - lieve what you
Chorus:
w/Rhy. Fig. 1
F♯m
A5
E
wan - na be - lieve. You see you don't have to live like a ref - u - gee.
F♯m
To Coda
A5
E
Don't have to live like a ref - u - gee.
Fill 1

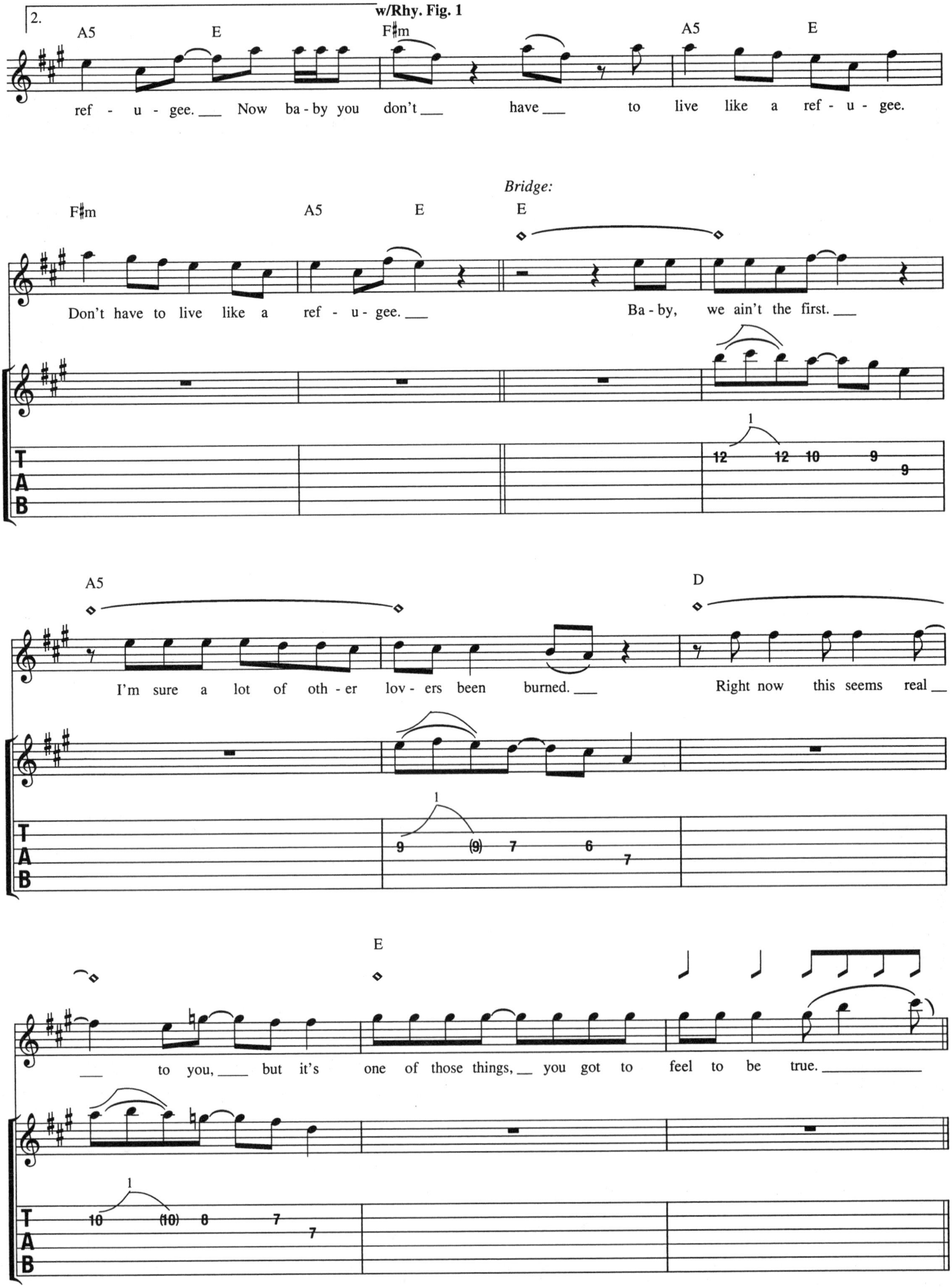
2.
w/Rhy. Fig. 1
A5 E F♯m A5 E
ref - u - gee. Now ba - by you don't have to live like a ref - u - gee.
F♯m A5 E
Bridge:
E
Don't have to live like a ref - u - gee. Ba - by, we ain't the first.
12 12 10 9 9
A5 D
I'm sure a lot of oth - er lov - ers been burned. Right now this seems real
9 (9) 7 6 7
E
to you, but it's one of those things, you got to feel to be true.
10 (10) 8 7 7

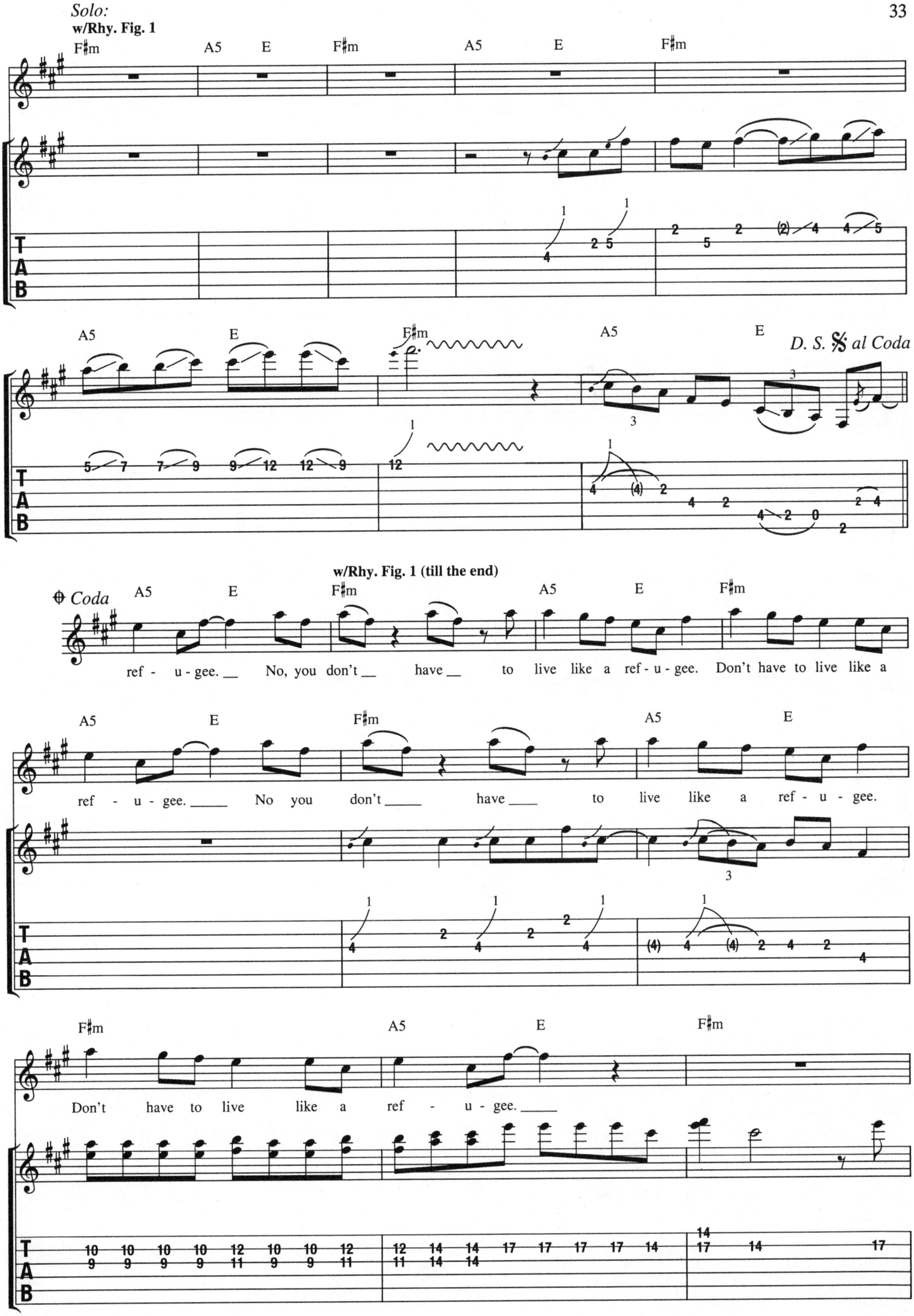
Solo:
w/Rhy. Fig. 1
F♯m A5 E F♯m A5 E F♯m
A5 E F♯m A5 E
D. S. 𝄋 al Coda
w/Rhy. Fig. 1 (till the end)
⊕ Coda
A5 E F♯m A5 E F♯m
ref - u - gee. No, you don't have to live like a ref - u - gee. Don't have to live like a
A5 E F♯m A5 E
ref - u - gee. No you don't have to live like a ref - u - gee.
F♯m A5 E F♯m
Don't have to live like a ref - u - gee.

Verse 2:
Somewhere, somehow, somebody must have
Kicked you around some.
Tell me, why you wanna lay there,
Revel in your abandon.
It don't make no difference to me, baby,
Everybody's had to fight to be free.
(To Chorus:)

Verse 3:
Somewhere, somehow, somebody must have
Kicked you around some.
Who knows, maybe you were kidnapped, tied up,
Taken away and held for ransom.
It don't really matter to me, baby,
Everybody's had to fight to be free.
(To Chorus:)

DON'T DO ME LIKE THAT

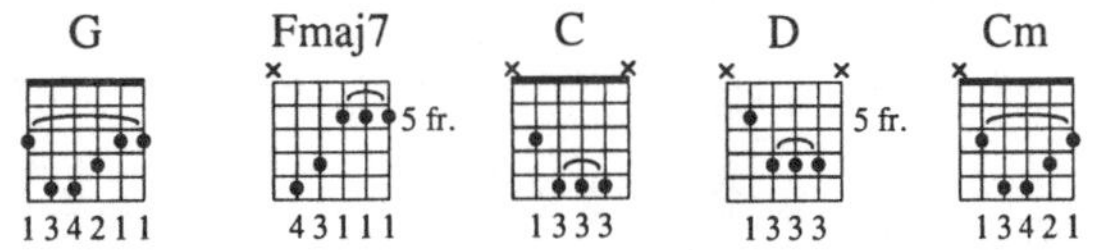

Words and Music by
TOM PETTY

Moderate rock ♩ = 114
Intro:

Chorus:
Rhy. Fig. 2
G
Fmaj7
Em
Gtr. 1
Don't do me like that, don't do me like that. What if I loved you ba - by;
Gtr. 2
T
A
B
C
D
(end Rhy. Fig. 2)
w/Rhy. Fig. 2
G
Fmaj7
don't do me like that. Don't do me like that, don't do me like that.
Gtr. 1
Gtr. 2
Em
C
D
To Coda
Some - day I might need you, ba - by; don't do me like that. ('Cause)
What if I
Gtr. 1
Bridge:
G
W/Fill 1
G
Some- where deep down in - side some - one is say - in', "Love does - n't last that
Fill 1
T
A
B

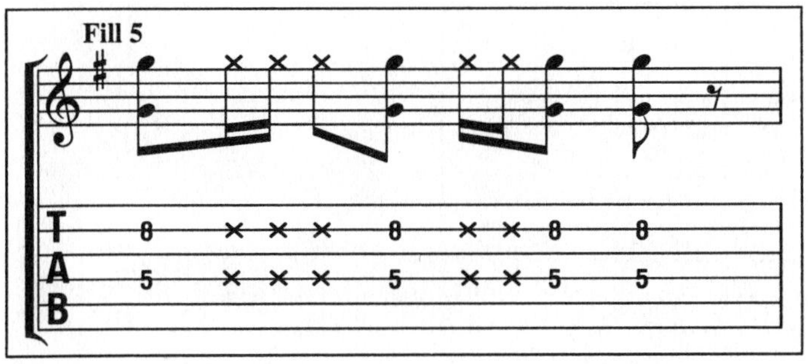

Verses 2 & 3:
Listen honey can't you see?
Baby it would bury me
If you were in the public eye,
Givin' someone else a try.
Well you know you better watch your step,
Or you're gonna get hurt yourself.
Someone's gonna tell you lies,
Cut you down to size.
(To Chorus:)

EVEN THE LOSERS

Words and Music by
TOM PETTY

G
w/Fill 2 (2nd time)
stared at the moon. ___
And I
D A G D
w/Fill 3 (2nd time)
showed __ you stars __ you nev - er could see. ___
Babe, It could - n't have
D A C(9)
1.
2.
been that eas - y to for - get a - bout me.
2. Ba - by,
Ba - by, e - ven the los -
Chorus:
D A G D A G
- ers, ___
get luck, - y some - times. __
E - ven the los -
Fill 2
T
A
B
7 6 4 4
2
Fill 3
T
A
B
12 14

D A G
- ers, keep a lit - tle bit of pride, they get
luck - y some - times.
Solo: D A
To Coda
* last time
Ba - by, e - ven the los -
G A
D A G
D A G

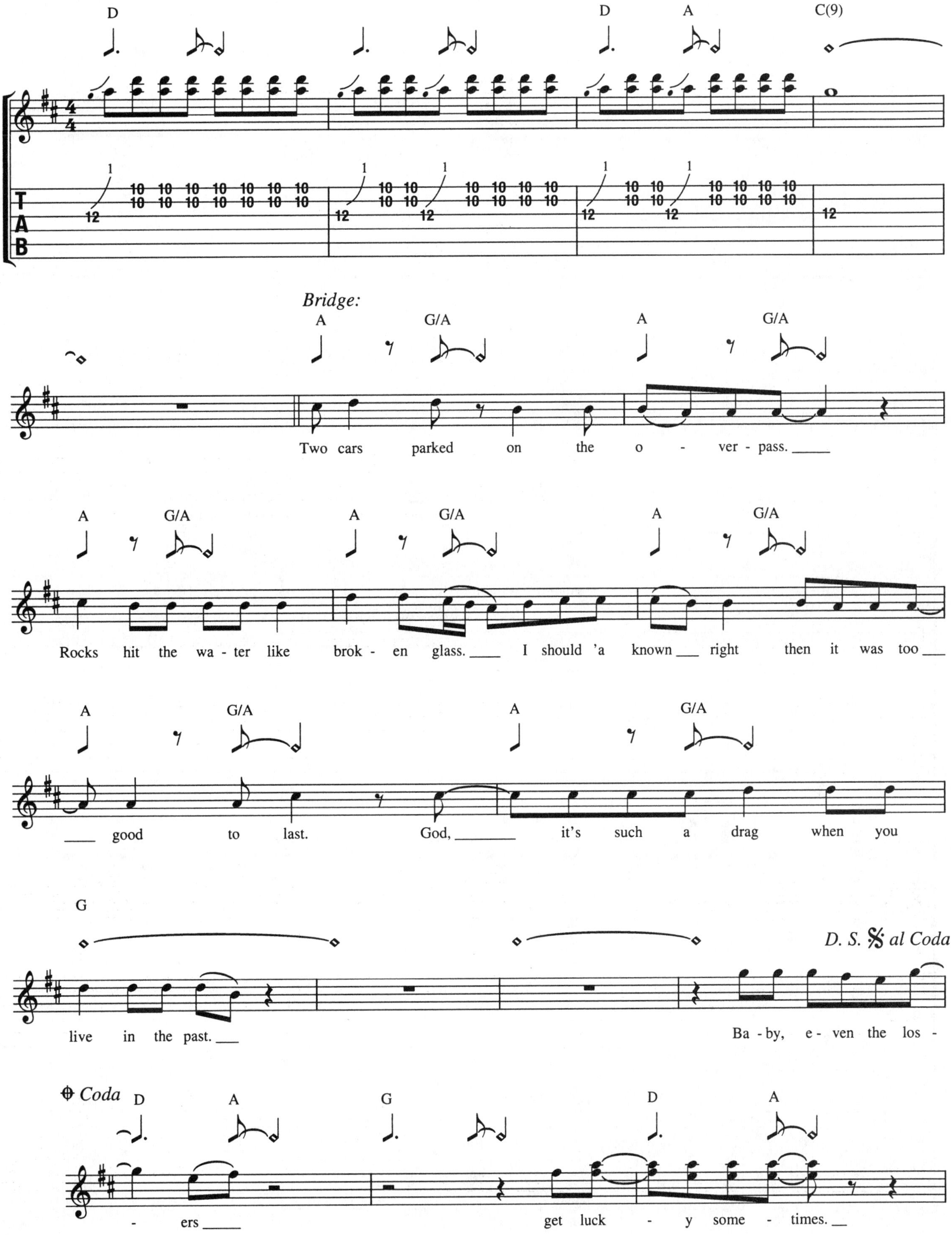
D
D A C(9)
T
A
B
Bridge:
A G/A A G/A
Two cars parked on the o - ver - pass. ____
A G/A A G/A A G/A
Rocks hit the wa - ter like brok - en glass. ____ I should 'a known ___ right then it was too ___
A G/A A G/A
___ good to last. God, _______ it's such a drag when you
G
D. S. 𝄋 al Coda
live in the past. ___ Ba - by, e - ven the los -
𝄌 Coda D A G D A
- ers _____ get luck - y some - times. __

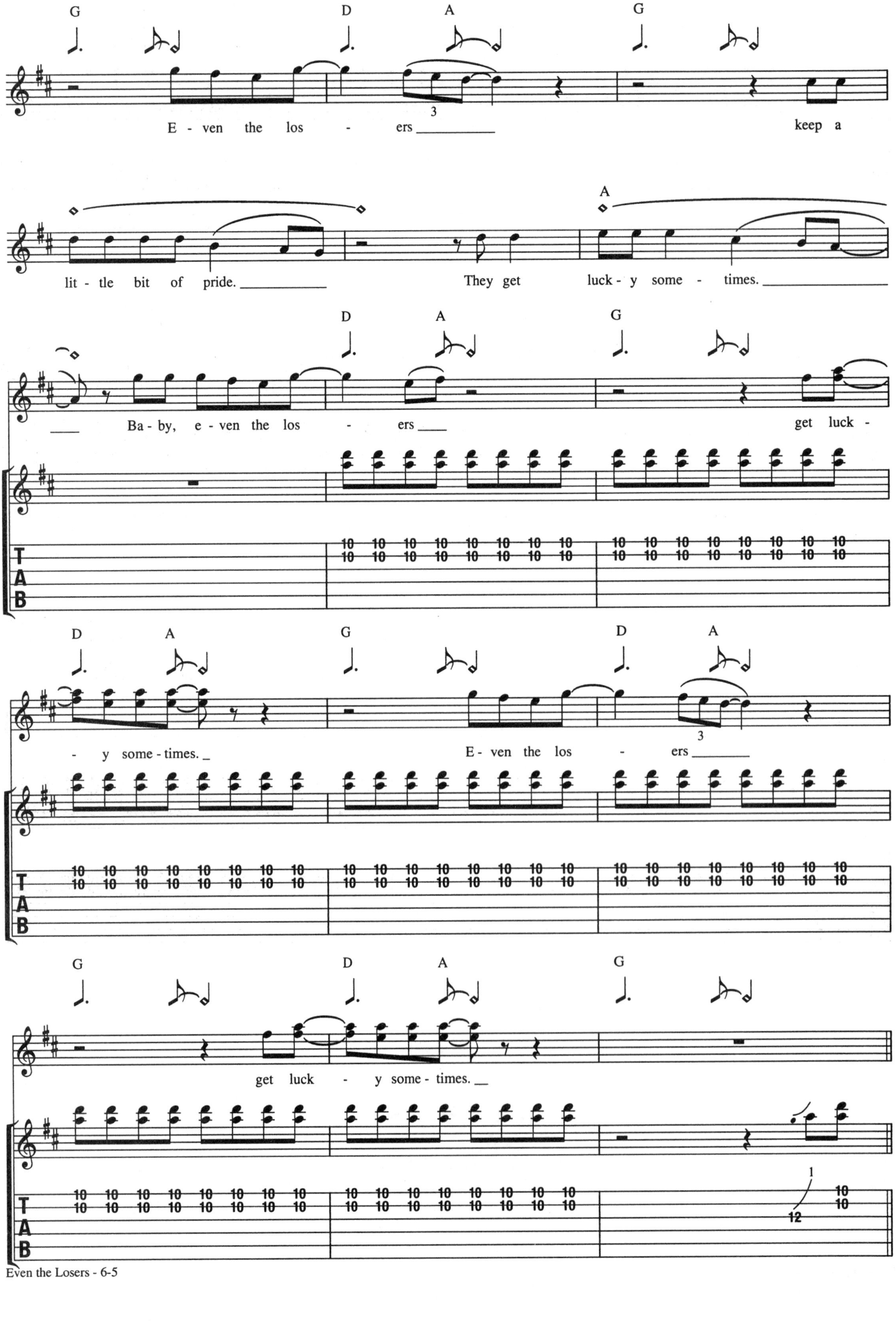
G D A G
E - ven the los - ers keep a
A
lit - tle bit of pride. They get luck - y some - times.
D A G
Ba - by, e - ven the los - ers get luck -
T
A
B
D A G D A
- y some - times. E - ven the los - ers
T
A
B
G D A G
get luck - y some - times.
T
A
B

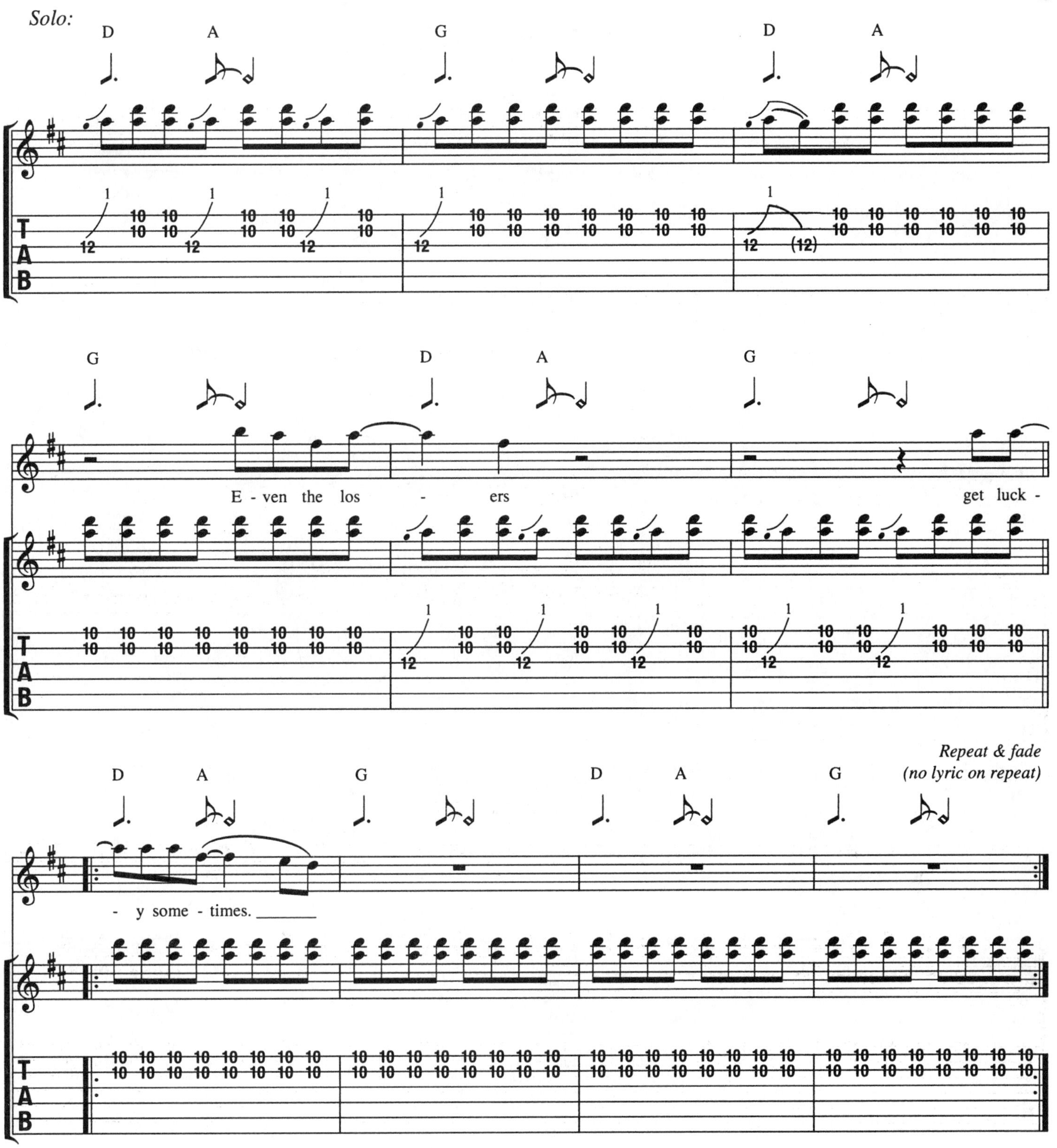

Verse 2:
Baby, time meant nothing
Anything seemed real.
Yeah, you could kiss like fire
And you made me feel
Like every word you said was
Meant to be.
It couldn't have been that easy
To forget about me.
(To Chorus:)

HERE COMES MY GIRL

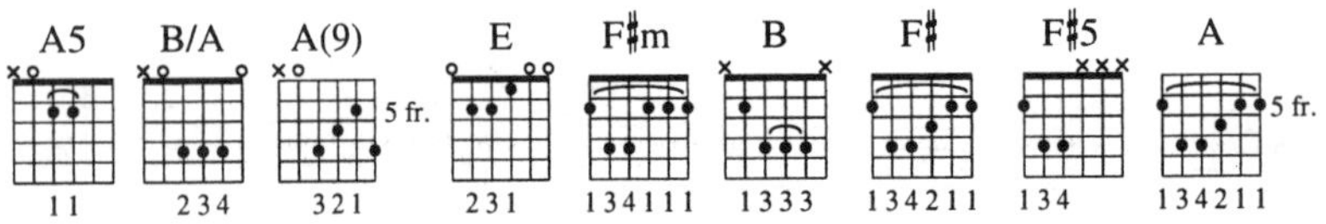

Words and Music by
TOM PETTY and MIKE CAMPBELL

Moderate rock ♩ = 106

Intro:

w/Rhy. Fig. 1, 1A & 1B (3 times)
A5
B/A
I ain't real-ly sure, but it seems I re - mem-ber the good times were just a lit-tle bit more
A(9)
B/A
A5
in fo - cus.
But when she puts her arms a - round me,
B/A
A(9)
B/A
I can some - how rise a - bove it.
A5
B/A
Yeah, ol' man when I got that lit - tle girl stand - in' right by my side, you know, I can
A(9)
B/A
tell the whole wide world to shove it, hey. Here comes my
Chorus:
E
A
girl. Here comes my
Rhy. Fig. 2
(end Rhy. Fig. 2)
TAB

w/Rhy. Fig. 2
E
A
w/Fill 1
F♯m
girl.
Yeah, she looks
B
To Coda
all right.
She is all I need to - night.
Bridge:
F♯5
w/Fill 2 (3 times)
D.S. al Coda
Watch her walk.
Coda
w/Rhy. Figs. 1 & 1B (twice)
A5
B/A
A
B/A
hold
Fill 1
hold
Fill 2

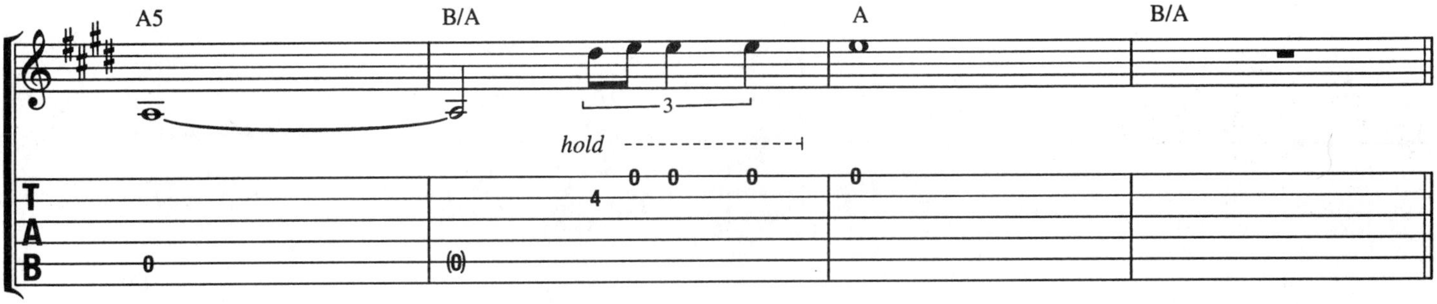

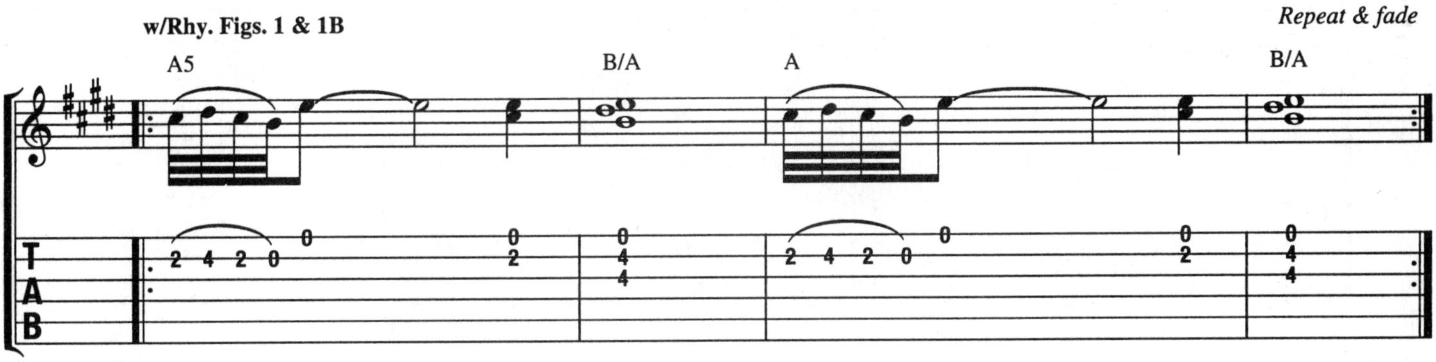

Verse 2:
Every now and then I get down to the end of the day,
I have to stop and ask myself why I've done it.
It just seems so useless to have to work so hard
And nothing ever really seems to come from it.
And then she looks me in the eye and says,
"We're gonna last forever."
Man, you know I can't begin to doubt it.
You know it just feels so good and so free and so right.
I know we ain't never gonna change our minds about it.
(To Chorus:)

Verse 3:
Every time it seems like there ain't nothin' left no more,
I find myself havin' to reach out and grab hold of something.
Then I just catch myself wondering, waiting and
Worrying about some silly little thing that don't add up to nothing.
And then she looks me in the eye and says,
"We're gonna last forever."
Man, you know I can't begin to doubt it.
You know it just feels so good and so free and so right,
I know we ain't never gonna change our minds about it.
(To Chorus:)

THE WAITING

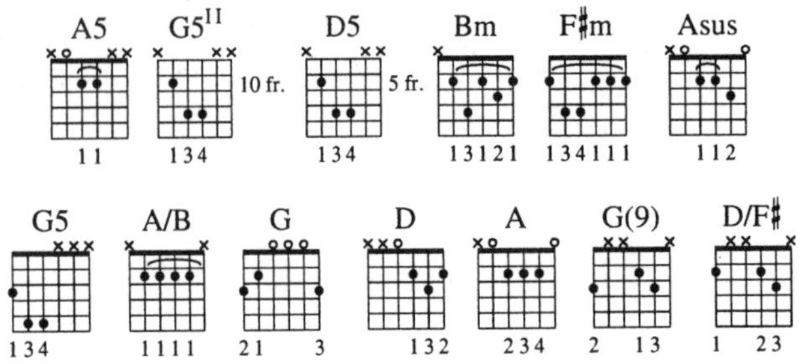

Words and Music by
TOM PETTY

A5 G5 D5 A5
feel like some - thin' from a dream? Yeah, I've nev - er known noth - in'
G5II D5 Bm
quite like this. Don't it feel like to - night might nev - er be a - gain? Ba - by,
G5 A5
we know bet - ter than to try and pre - tend. Hon - ey no one could - a ev - er
told me 'bout this. I said yeah, yeah, (yeah, yeah) yeah, yeah, yeah, yeah. The
Chorus: G D A D
wait - ing is the hard - est part.
hold
G D A D
Ev - 'ry day you see one more card. You
get one more yard.
(hold)

3rd time w/Fill 2 (4 times)
G D A D G D
take it on faith, you take it to the heart.___ The wait - ing is the
A D
w/Fill 1 (3rd time w/Fill 3)
To Coda
1.
hard - est part.
2. Well,
2.
Bridge:
Bm A/B Bm A/B
Oh, don't let 'em kill you babe, don't let 'em get to you.
Fill 2
Fill 3

Bm A/B Bm A/B A5
Don't let 'em kill you babe, don't let 'em get to you. I'll be your bleed - in' heart,
D5 G5 F♯m
I'll be your cry - in' fool. Don't let this go too far, don't let it get to you.
Solo:
A5 G5II D5 A5
G5 D5 A5 G5II D5

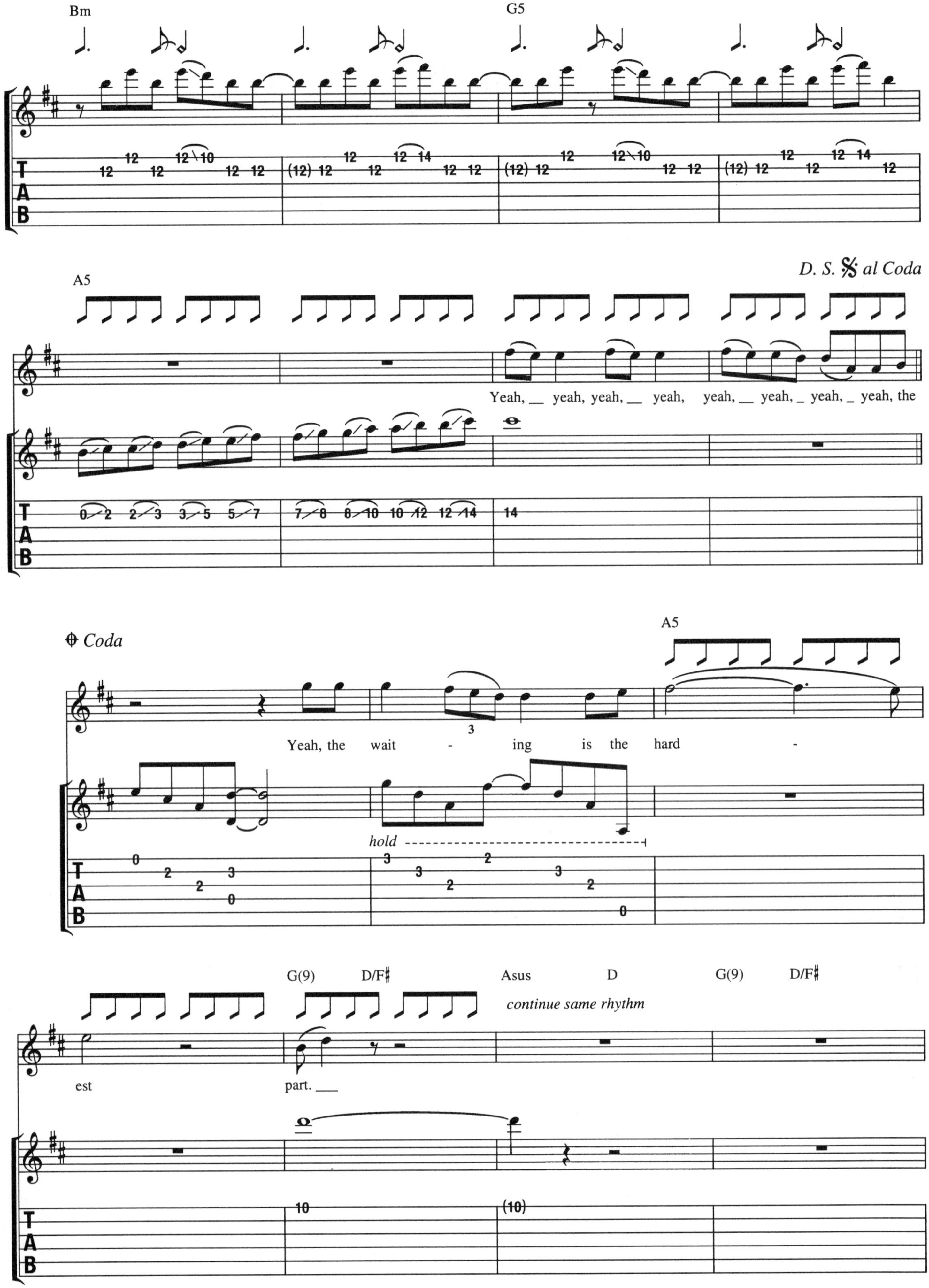
Bm
G5
A5
D. S. 𝄋 al Coda
Yeah, yeah, yeah, yeah, yeah, yeah, yeah, yeah, yeah, the
𝄌 Coda
A5
Yeah, the wait - ing is the hard -
hold
G(9) D/F♯ Asus D G(9) D/F♯
continue same rhythm
est part.
T A B

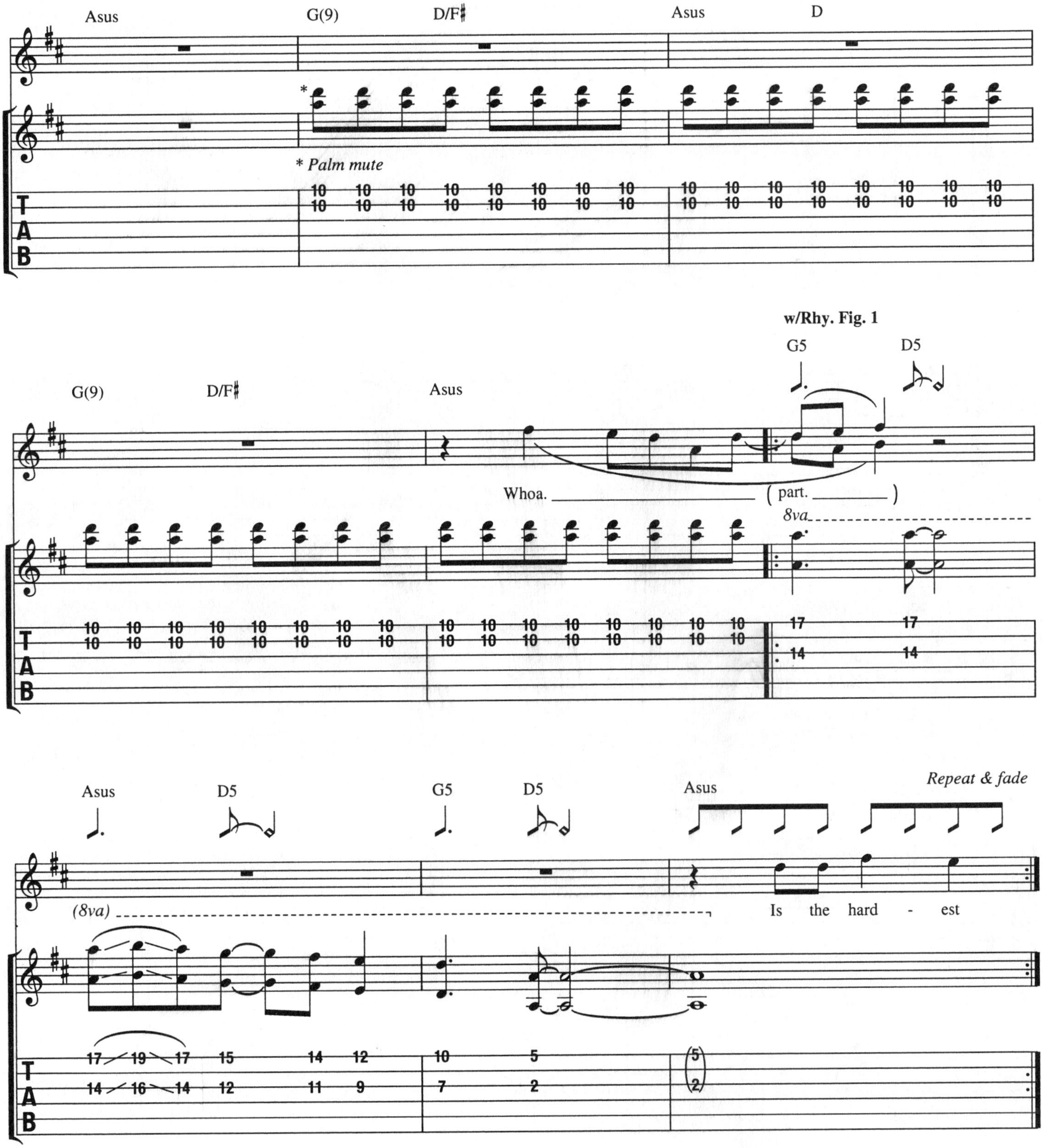

Verse 2:
Well, yeah I might have chased a couple of women around.
Oh, all it ever got me was down.
Yeah, then there were those that made me feel good,
But never as good as I'm feelin' right now.
Baby you're the only one that's ever known how
To make me want to live like I want to live.
Now I said yeah, yeah, (yeah, yeah)
yeah, yeah, yeah, yeah, . . .
(To Chorus:)

YOU GOT LUCKY

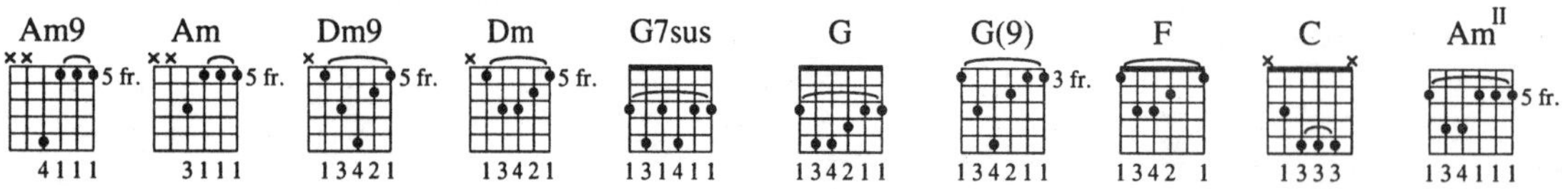

Words and Music by
TOM PETTY and MIKE CAMPBELL

Moderate rock ♩ = 114

Intro:

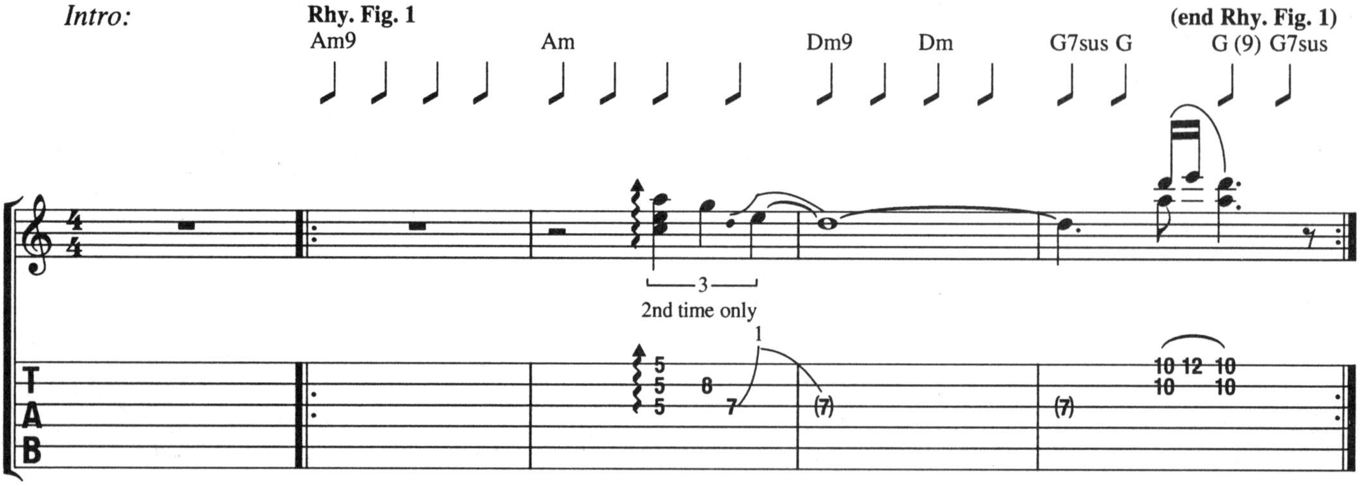

Verses 1 & 2:

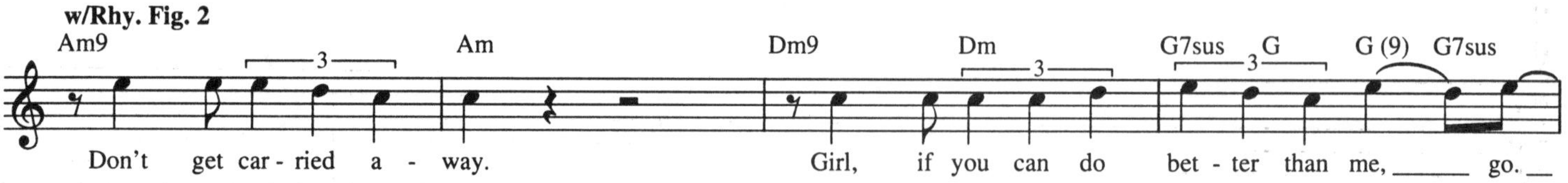

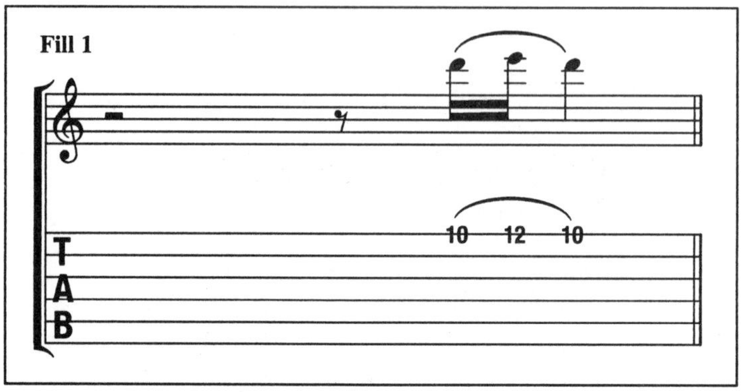

w/Fill 2 (2nd time)
Am^II
F
Yeah ___ go, ___
but re - mem - ber:
w/trem. bar
*3rd time only
Chorus:
C
Am^II
Good __ love ___ is hard to find.
Good __ love ___ is hard to find. ___ You got __
F
G
To Coda
luck - y ___ babe, __ you got __ luck - y babe, __ when I found __ you. _
1. w/Rhy. Figs. 1 & 2
Am9
Am
Dm9
Dm
G7sus
G
G(9)
G7sus
Fill 2
hold

Guitar Solo:

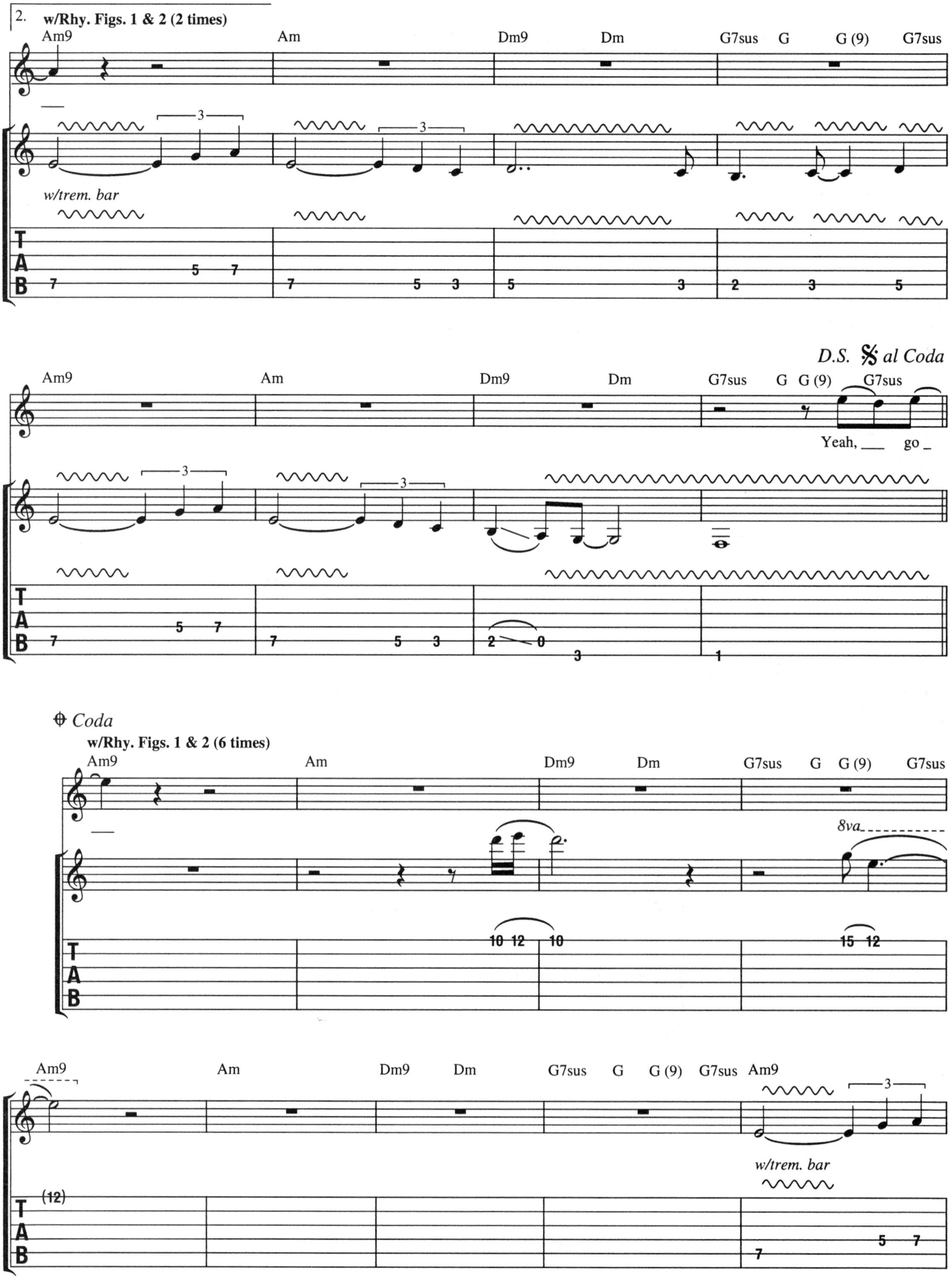
2.
w/Rhy. Figs. 1 & 2 (2 times)
Am9 Am Dm9 Dm G7sus G G (9) G7sus
w/trem. bar
D.S. 𝄋 al Coda
Am9 Am Dm9 Dm G7sus G G (9) G7sus
Yeah, ___ go _
⊕ Coda
w/Rhy. Figs. 1 & 2 (6 times)
Am9 Am Dm9 Dm G7sus G G (9) G7sus
8va
Am9 Am Dm9 Dm G7sus G G (9) G7sus Am9
w/trem. bar

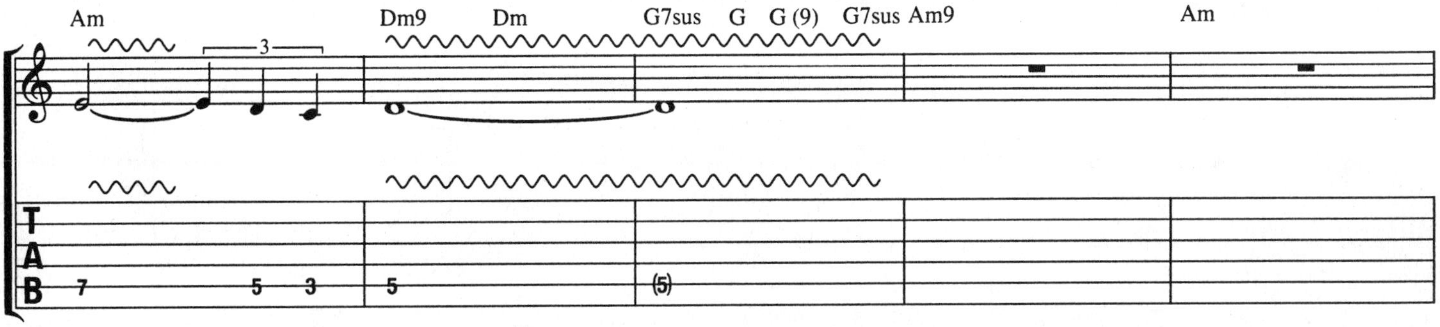

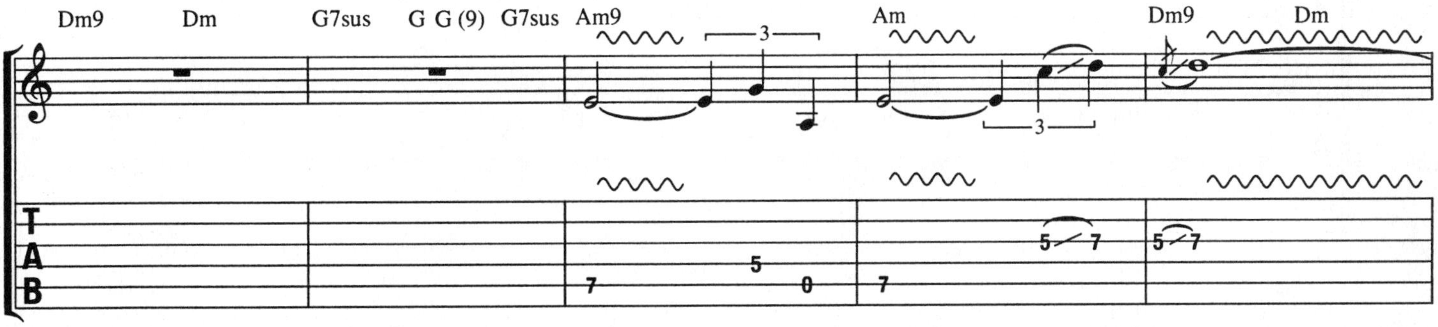

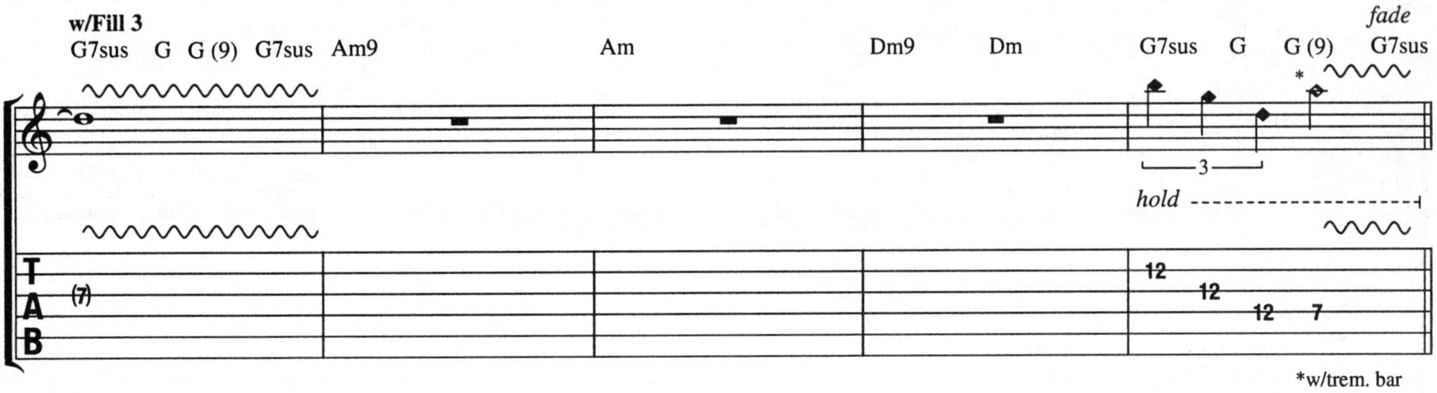

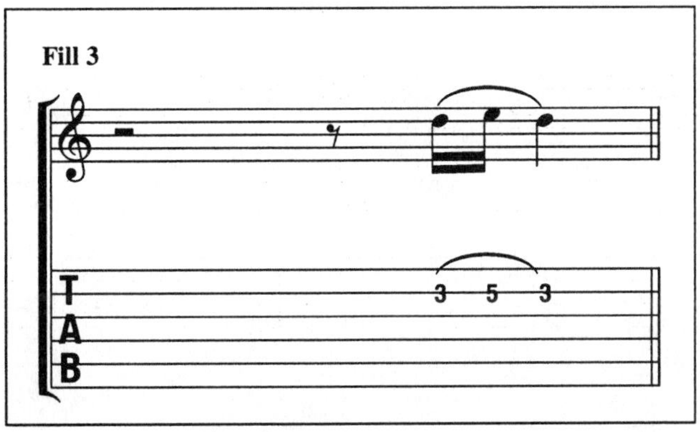

Verse2:
You put a hand on my cheek,
And then you turn your eyes away.
If you don't feel complete,
If I don't take you all of the way then go.
Yeah go, but remember:
(To Chorus:)

DON'T COME AROUND HERE NO MORE

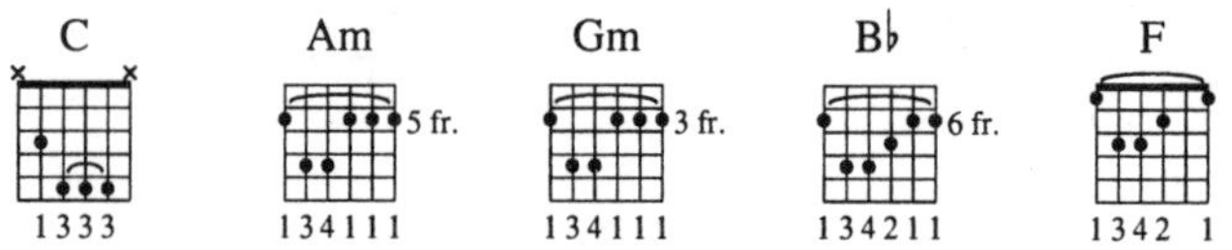

Words and Music by
TOM PETTY and DAVID A. STEWART

Slow rock ♩ = 80
Intro:

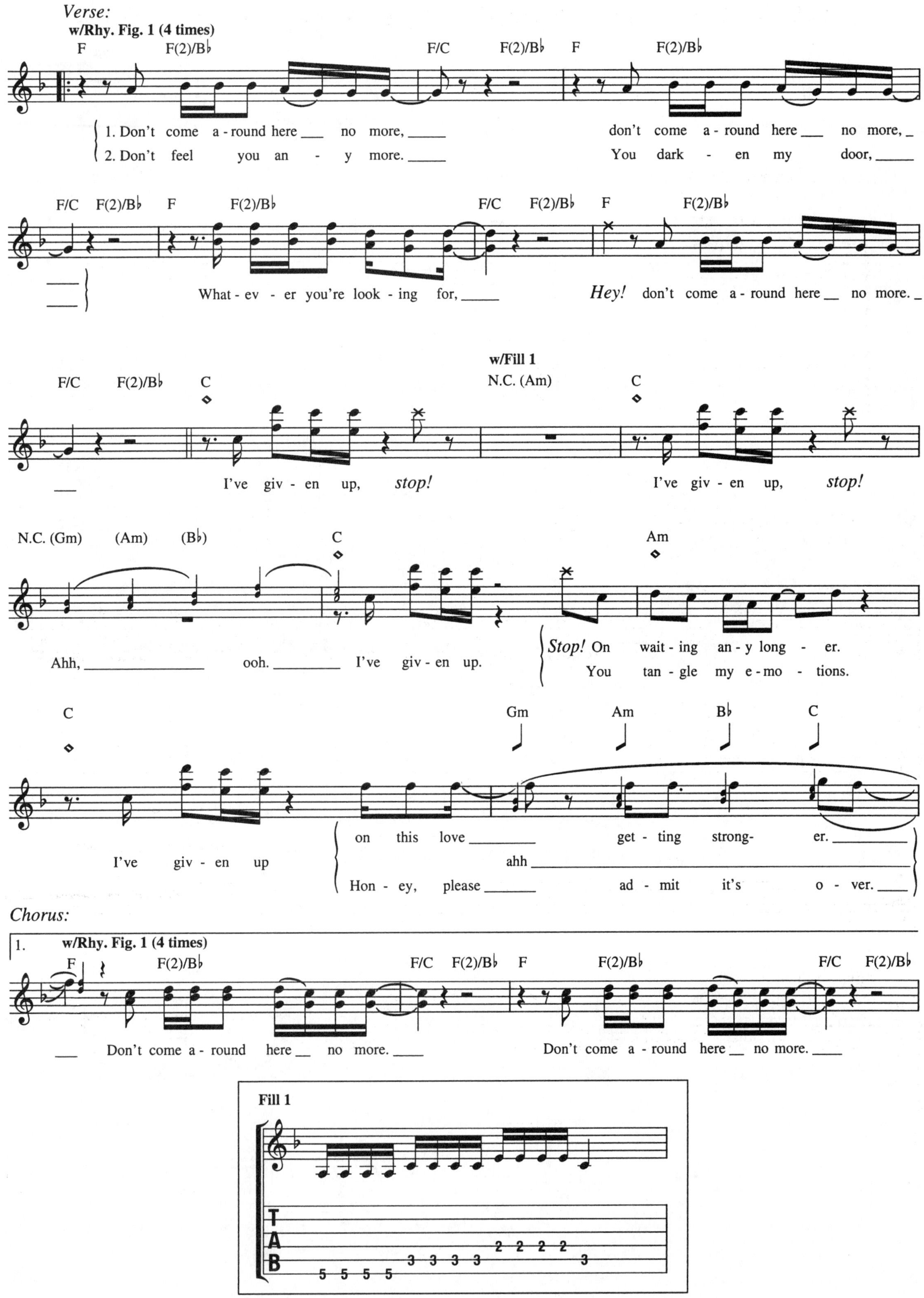
Verse:
w/Rhy. Fig. 1 (4 times)
F F(2)/B♭ F/C F(2)/B♭ F F(2)/B♭
1. Don't come a - round here ___ no more, ___ don't come a - round here ___ no more, _
2. Don't feel you an - y more. ___ You dark - en my door, ___
F/C F(2)/B♭ F F(2)/B♭ F/C F(2)/B♭ F F(2)/B♭
What - ev - er you're look - ing for, ___ Hey! don't come a - round here __ no more. _
F/C F(2)/B♭ C
w/Fill 1
N.C. (Am) C
I've giv - en up, stop! I've giv - en up, stop!
N.C. (Gm) (Am) (B♭) C Am
Ahh, ___ ooh. ___ I've giv - en up.
Stop! On wait - ing an - y long - er.
You tan - gle my e - mo - tions.
C Gm Am B♭ C
I've giv - en up
on this love ___ get - ting strong- er. ___
ahh ___
Hon - ey, please ___ ad - mit it's o - ver. ___
Chorus:
1.
w/Rhy. Fig. 1 (4 times)
F F(2)/B♭ F/C F(2)/B♭ F F(2)/B♭ F/C F(2)/B♭
Don't come a - round here __ no more. ___ Don't come a - round here __ no more. ___
Fill 1
T
A
B
5 5 5 5 3 3 3 3 2 2 2 2 3

F F(2)/B♭ F/C F(2)/B♭ F F(2)/B♭ F/C F(2)/B♭
Don't come a - round here no more. Don't come a - round here no more.
2.
F F
Ahh
Hey!
T
A
B
5 6 6 5 5 6 6 5 5 6 6 5 6 6 8 6 5 6 6
w/Rhy. Fig. 1 (4 times)
F F(2)/B♭ F/C F(2)/B♭ F F(2)/B♭ F/C F(2)/B♭
Don't come a - round here no more. Don't come a - round here no more
F F(2)/B♭ F/C F(2)/B♭ F F(2)/B♭ F/C F(2)/B♭
Don't come a - round here no more. Don't come a - round here no more
Verse:
F5 F5/B♭ C B♭ F5 F5/B♭ C D
3. Stop walk - ing down my street. Don't come a - round here no more
F5 F(5)/B♭ C D F5 F(5)/B♭ C D
Who you ex - pect to meet? Don't come a - round here no more

F5 F5/B♭ C D F5 F5/B♭ C D
What - ev - er you're look - ing for, Hey! don't come a - round here no more.
Double - time feel ♪ = ♩
Rhy. Fig. 2
(end Rhy. Fig. 2)
F F/B♭ C B♭
Solo:
w/Rhy. Fig. 2
F *(B♭) (C) (B♭)
Please, don't come a - round here no more.
*w/wah wah
*Indicates bass line
F (B♭) (C) (B♭)
What - ev - er you're look - in'

F (B♭) (C) (B♭) F
for.
(B♭) (C) (B♭) F (B♭) (C)
(B♭) F (B♭) (C)
Don't come a - round here no more.
(B♭) F (B♭) (C) (B♭)
fade
8va

I WON'T BACK DOWN

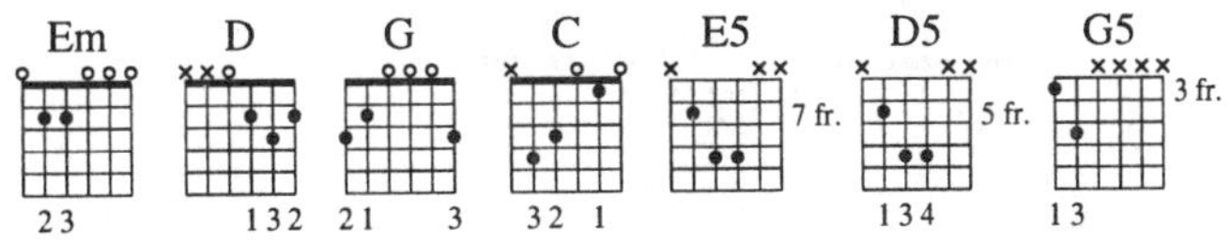

Words and Music by
TOM PETTY and JEFF LYNNE

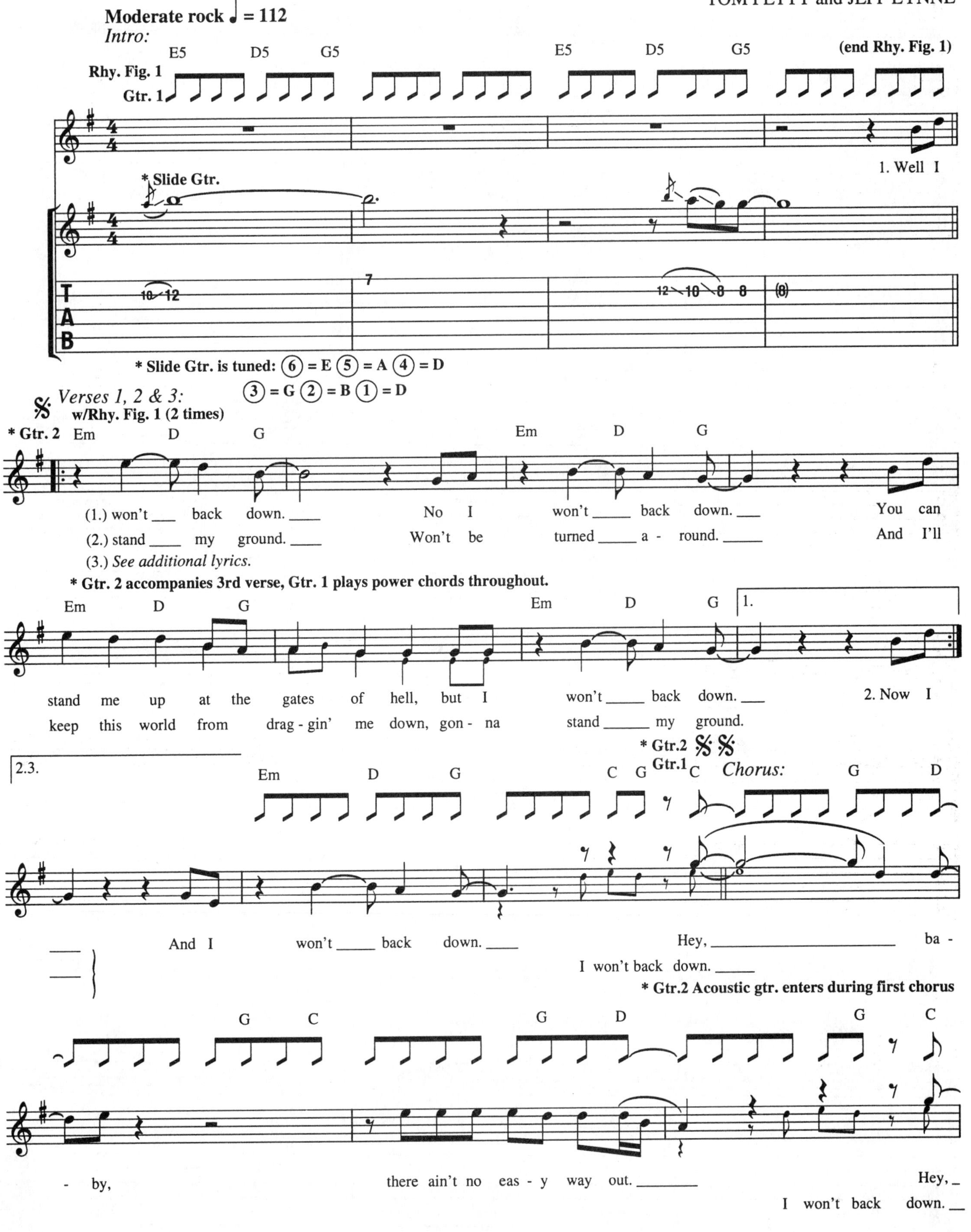

To Coda
G D
w/Rhy. Fig. 1
Em D G
1.
I
will stand my ground, and I
Em D G
D. S.
2.
w/Rhy. Fig. 1 (3 times)
Em D G
won't back down.
3. Well, I
and I won't back down.
I wont back down.
Guitar Solo:
Em Dm G
Em D G
Slide Gtr.
Em D G
Em D G
D. S. S. al Coda
Em D G
C G C
Hey,
I won't back down.

Verse 3:
Well, I know what's right.
I got just one life.
In a world that keeps on pushin' me around.
But I'll stand my ground.
And I won't back down.
(To Chorus:)

RUNNIN' DOWN A DREAM

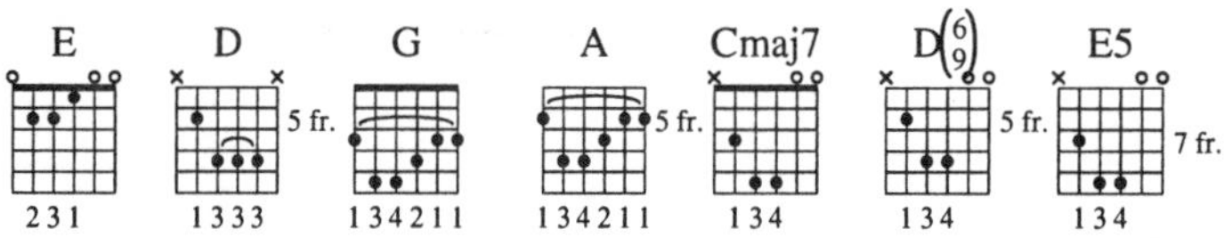

Words and Music by
TOM PETTY, MIKE CAMPBELL
and JEFF LYNNE

*Gtr. 3 is an acoustic guitar

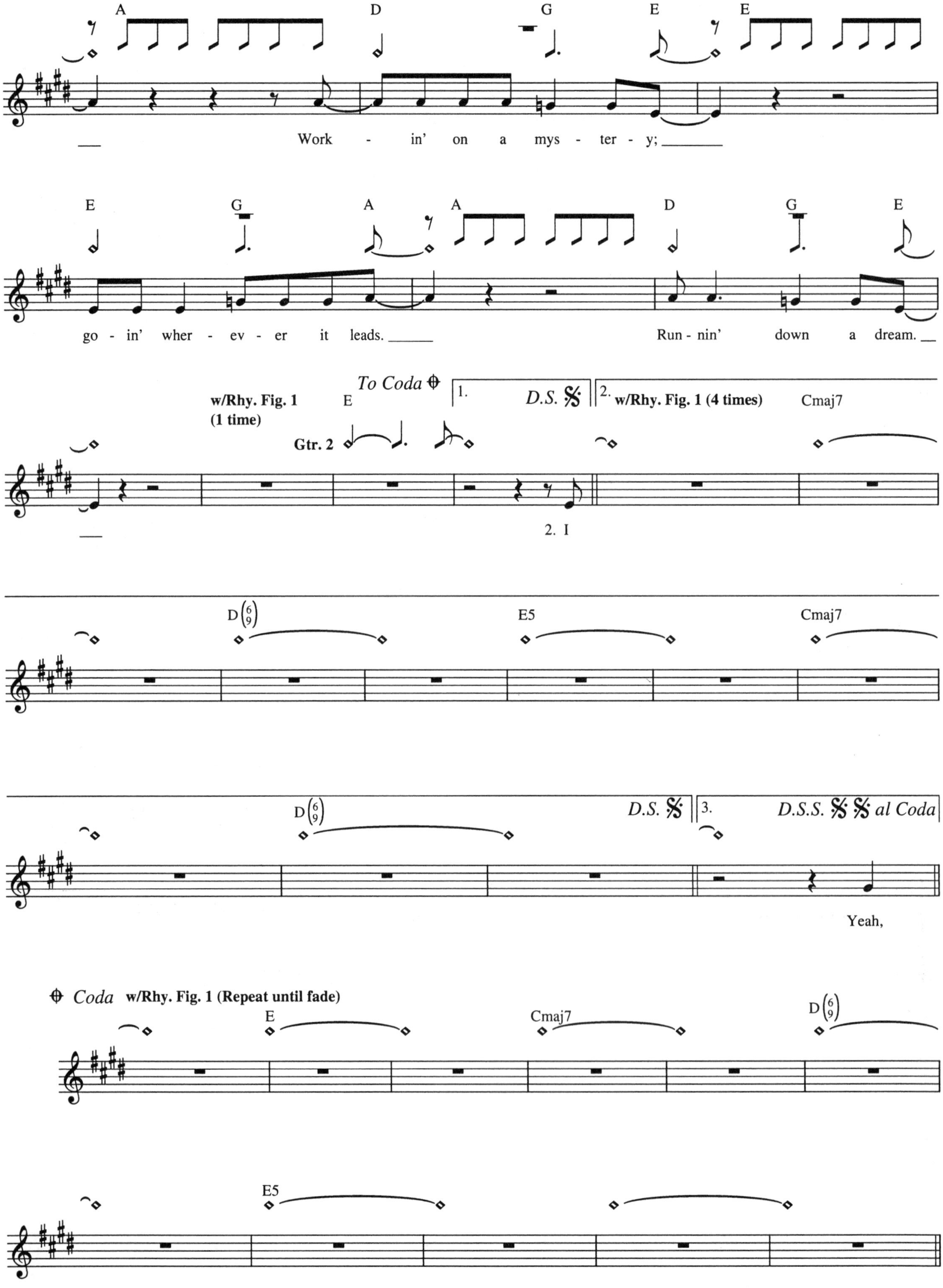
A
D
G
E
E
Work - in' on a mys - ter - y;
E
G
A
A
D
G
E
go - in' wher - ev - er it leads.
Run - nin' down a dream.
To Coda
w/Rhy. Fig. 1
(1 time)
E
Gtr. 2
1.
D.S.
2. w/Rhy. Fig. 1 (4 times)
Cmaj7
2. I
D(6/9)
E5
Cmaj7
D(6/9)
D.S.
3.
D.S.S. al Coda
Yeah,
Coda w/Rhy. Fig. 1 (Repeat until fade)
E
Cmaj7
D(6/9)
E5

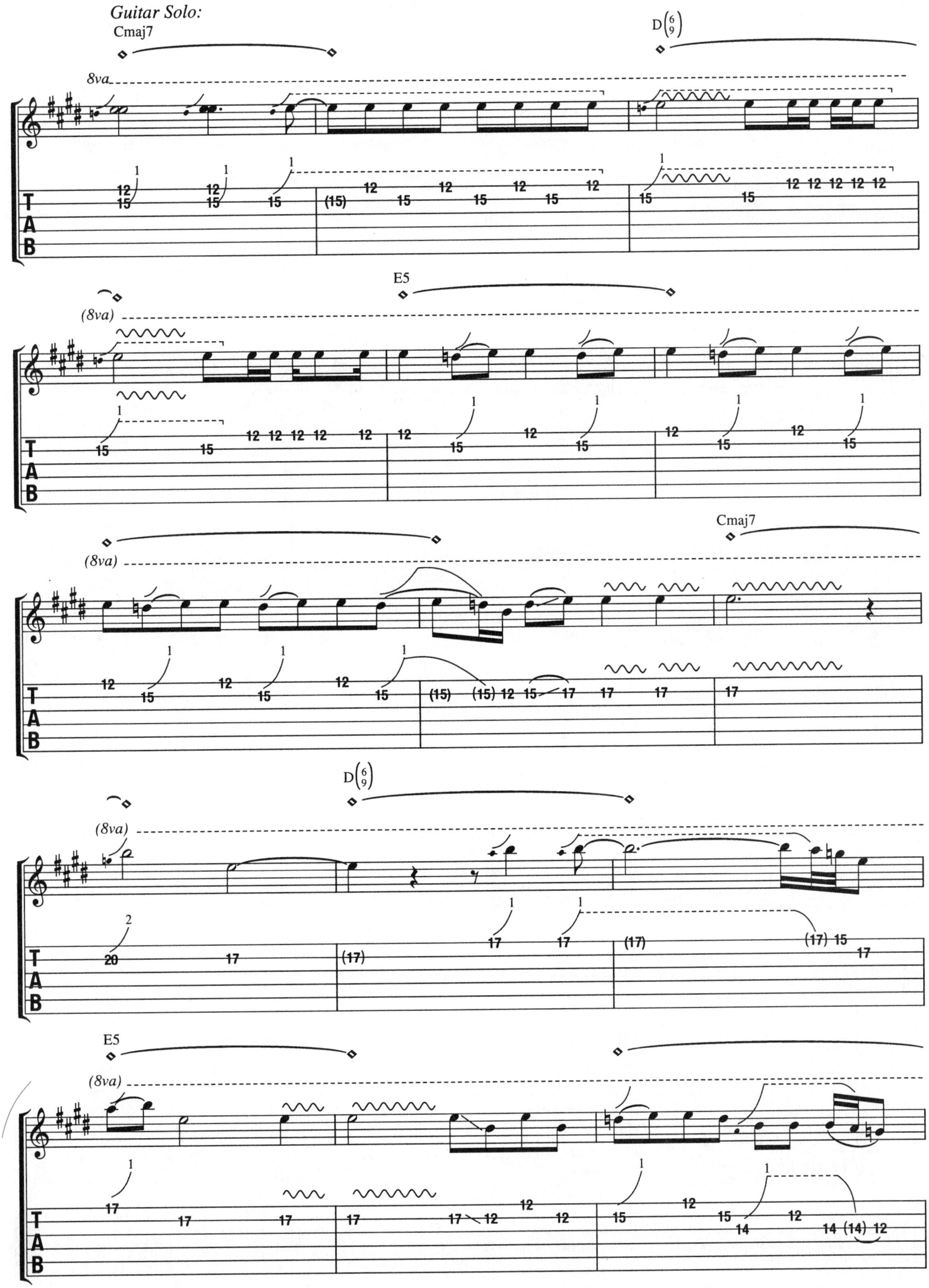
Guitar Solo:
Cmaj7
D(6/9)
8va
E5
(8va)
Cmaj7
D(6/9)
E5
T
A
B

Cmaj7
(8va)
Dadd(6/9)
E5
(8va)
(8va)
Cmaj7
Dadd(6/9)
(8va)
E5
(8va)

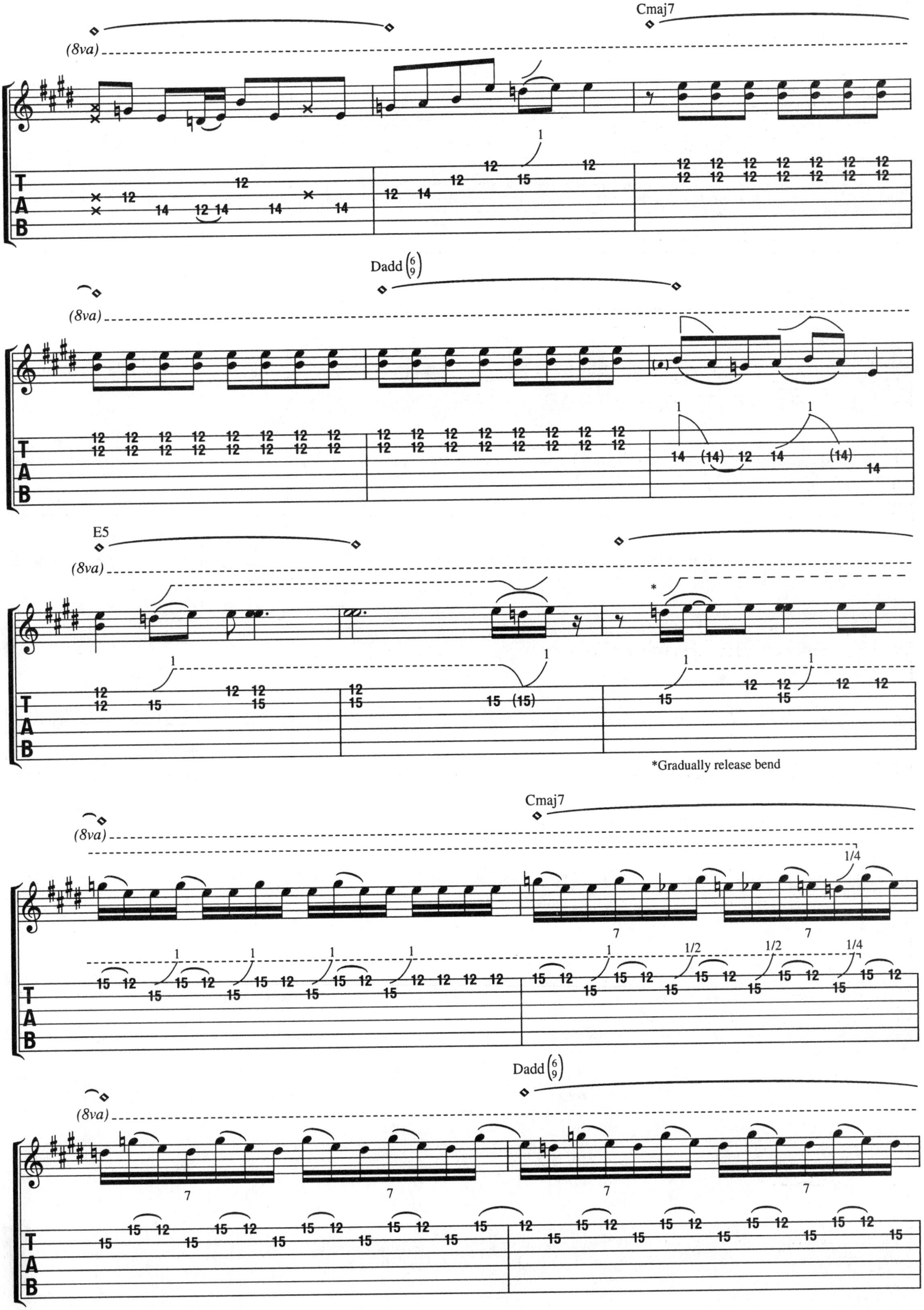
Cmaj7
(8va)
Dadd(6 9)
(8va)
E5
(8va)
*Gradually release bend
Cmaj7
(8va)
Dadd(6 9)
(8va)

Verse 2:
I felt so good, like anything was possible.
Hit the cruise control and rubbed my eyes.
The last three days, the rain was unstoppable.
It was always cold, no sunshine.
(To Chorus:)

Verse 3:
I rolled on, the sky grew dark.
I put the pedal down to make some more time.
There's something good waitin' down this road.
I'm pickin' up whatever is mine.
(To Chorus:)

FREE FALLIN'

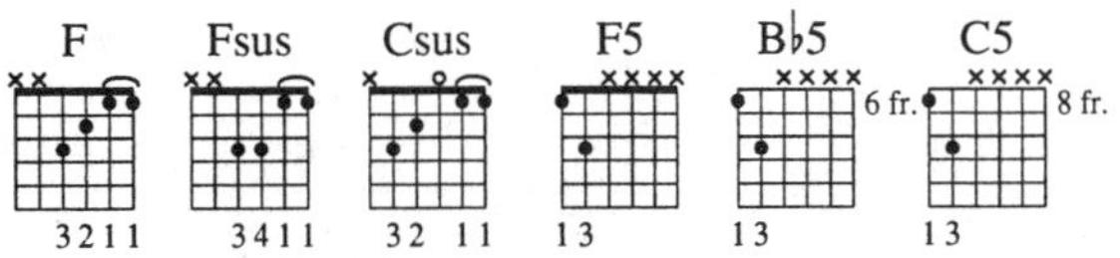

Words and Music by
TOM PETTY and JEFF LYNNE

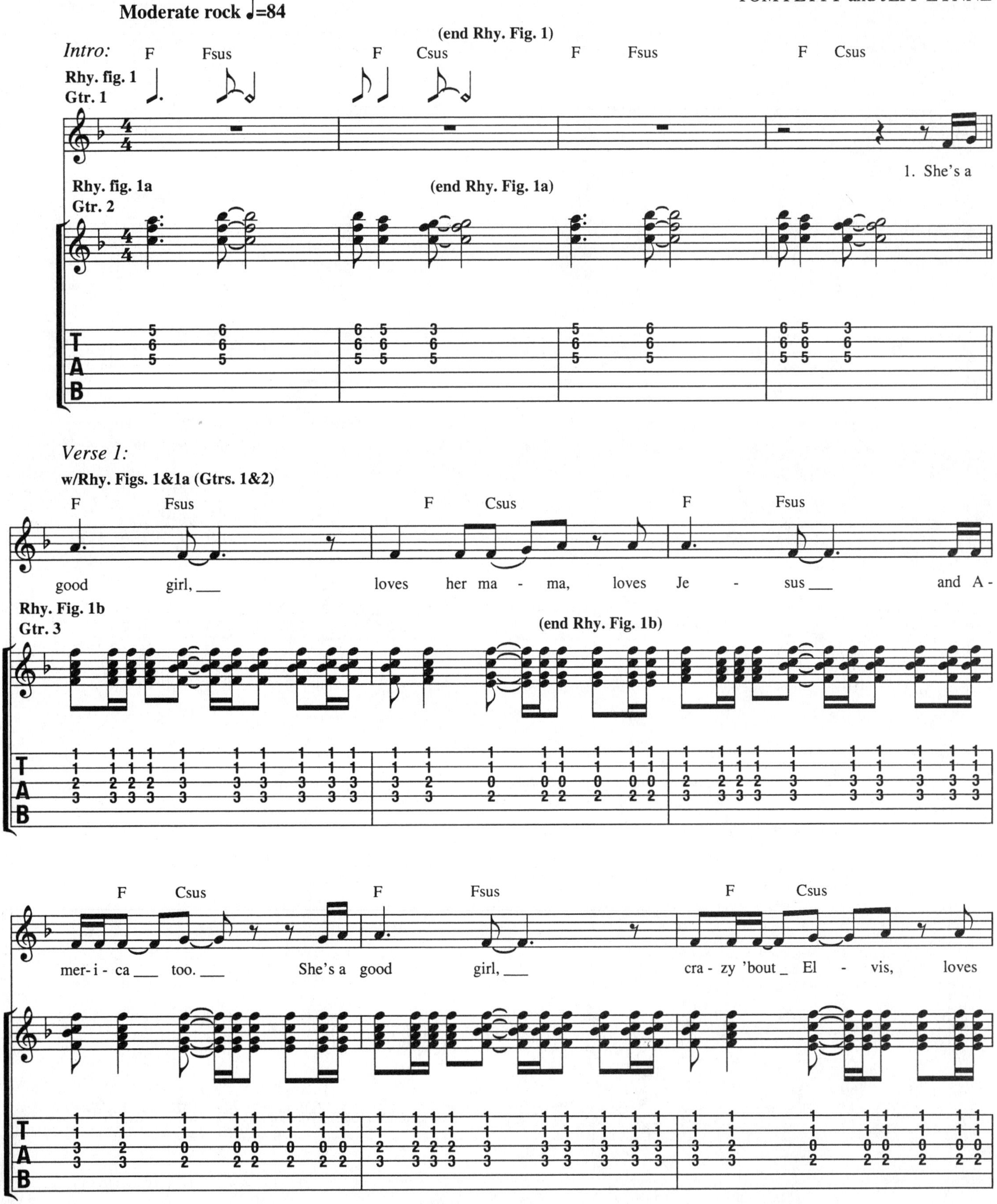

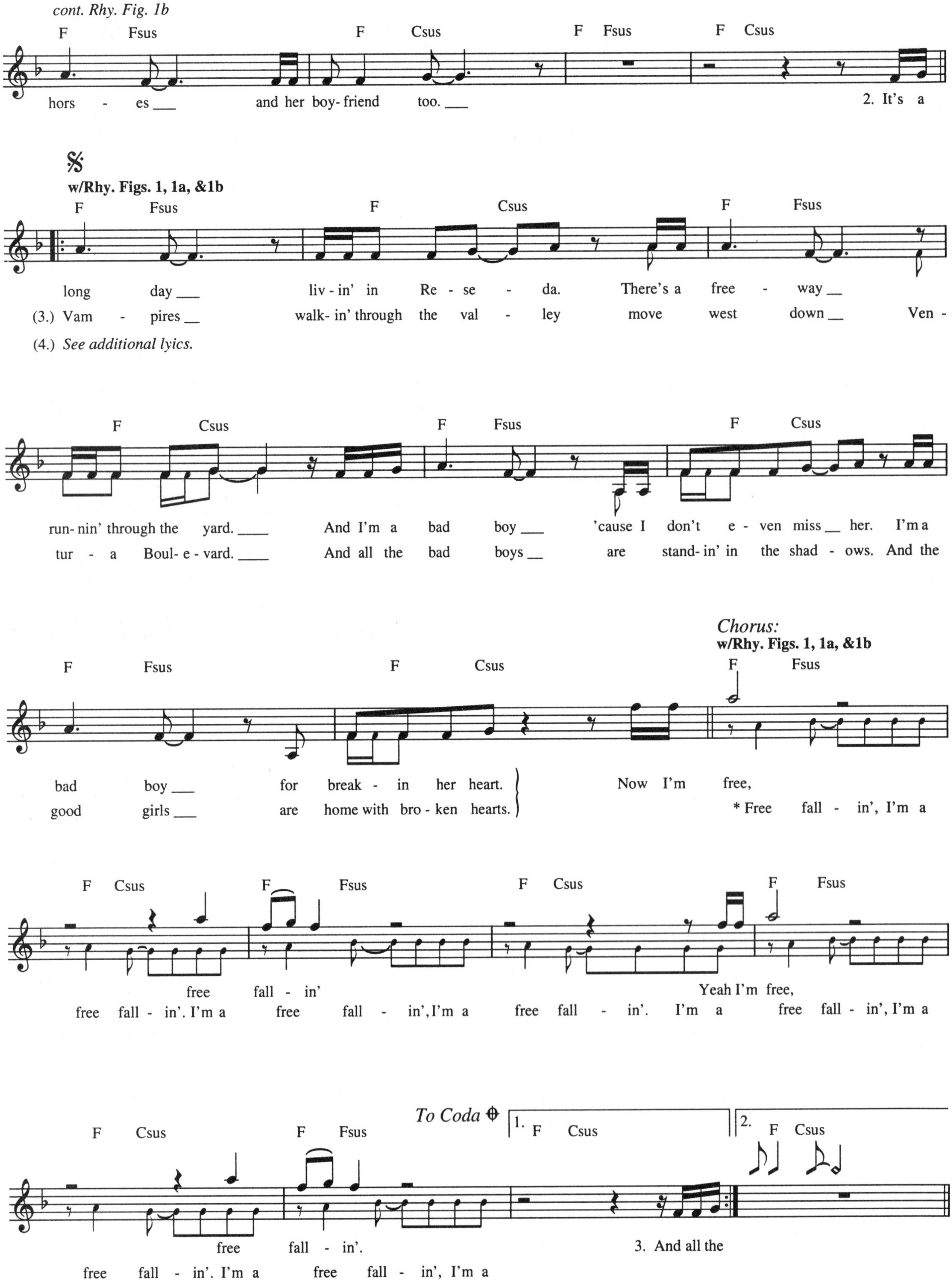

* Background vocals after 4th Verse.

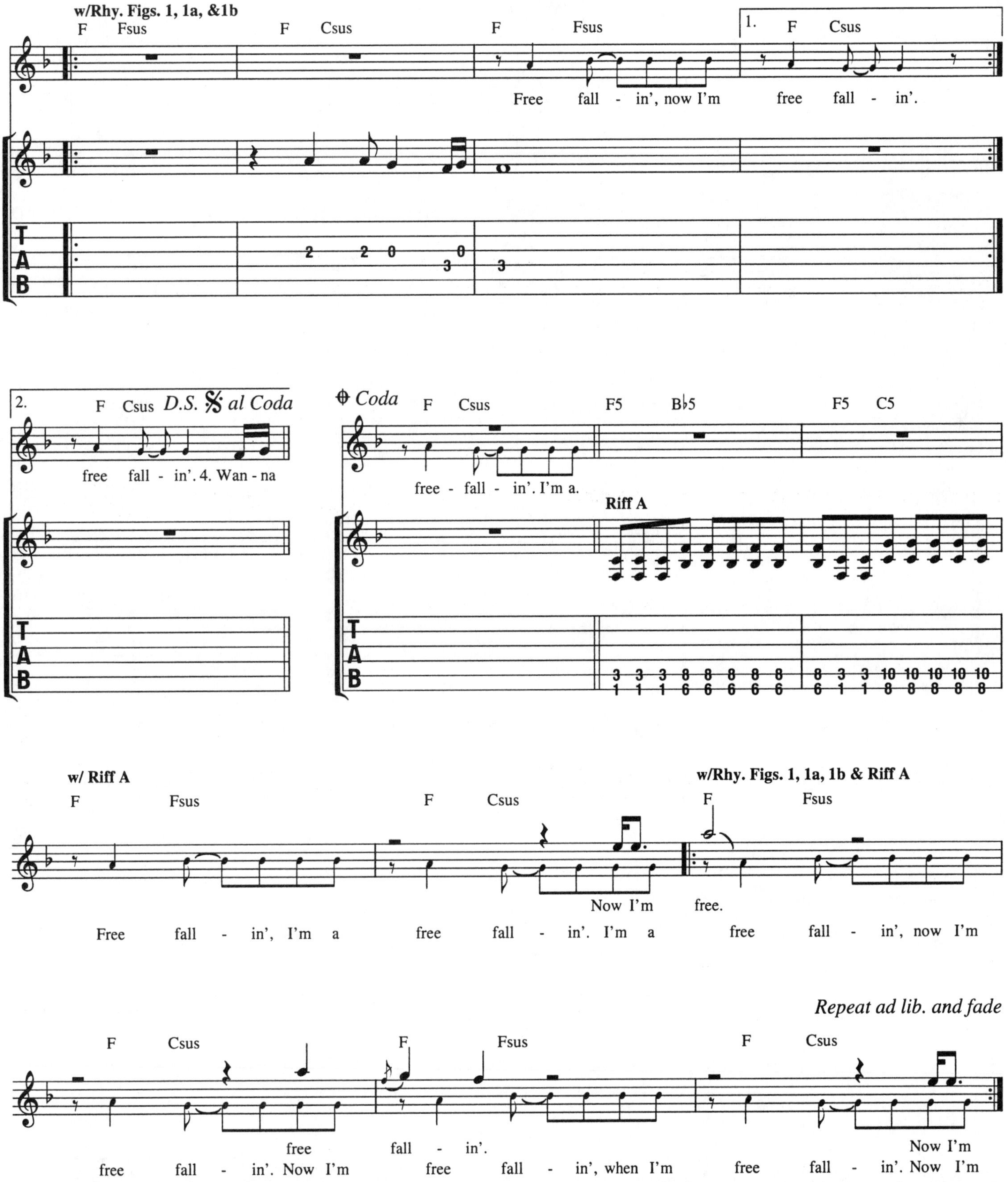

Verse 4:
I wanna glide down over Mulholland.
I wanna write her name in the sky.
I wanna free fall out into nothin'.
Gonna leave this world for awhile.
(To Chorus:)

LEARNING TO FLY

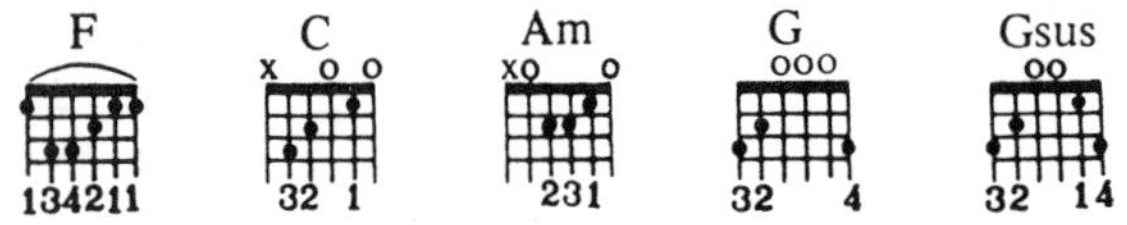

Words and Music by
TOM PETTY and JEFF LYNNE

Moderate rock ♩= 118

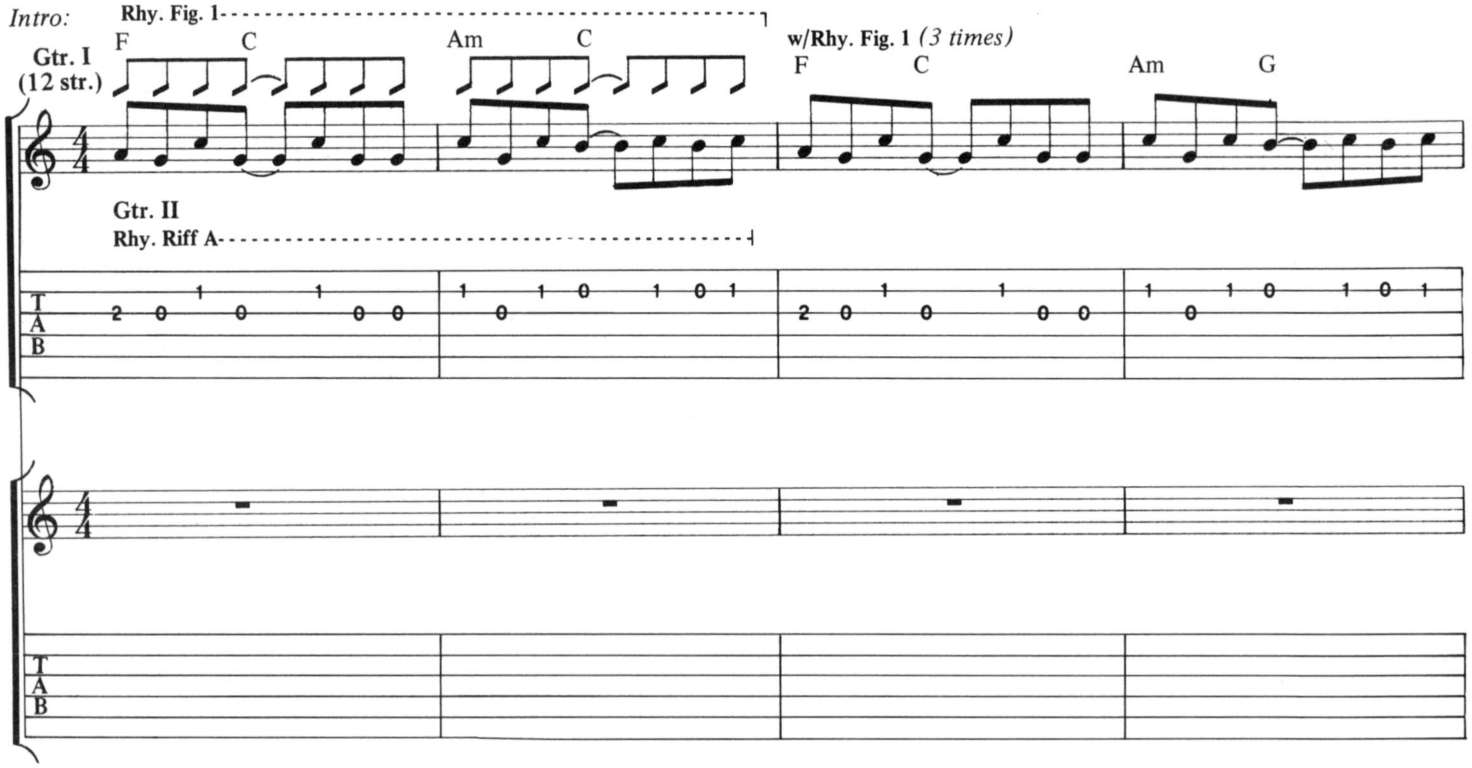

*Gtr. III staccato chords w/palm mute.

Verse 1:
w/Rhy. Riff A & Rhy. Figs. 1 & 1A (until Chorus)
F C Am G F C
start - ed out
down a dirt - y road.
Am G F C Am G
Start - ed out
Verses 2 & 3:
F C Am G C Am G
all a - lone.
And the sun went down
good ol' days,
as I
may
F C Am G F C
crossed the hill,
not re - turn,
and the town lit up,
and the rocks might melt
T
A
B
Am G F C Am G
the world got still.
and the sea may burn.
1.2. I'm
Gtr. II
T
A
B
8

Chorus:
w/Rhy. Figs. 1 & 1B (4 times)
F C Am G F C
learn - ing to fly
3. See additional lyrics (chorus 3)
Learn - ing to fly,
but I ain't got wings.
hold-
Rhy. Riff B
Am G F C Am G
learn - ing to fly,
Com - ing down
learn - ing to fly.
is the
F C
3rd time to Coda
1.
2.
hard - est thing.
3. Well the
learn - ing to fly.
(end Rhy. Riff B)

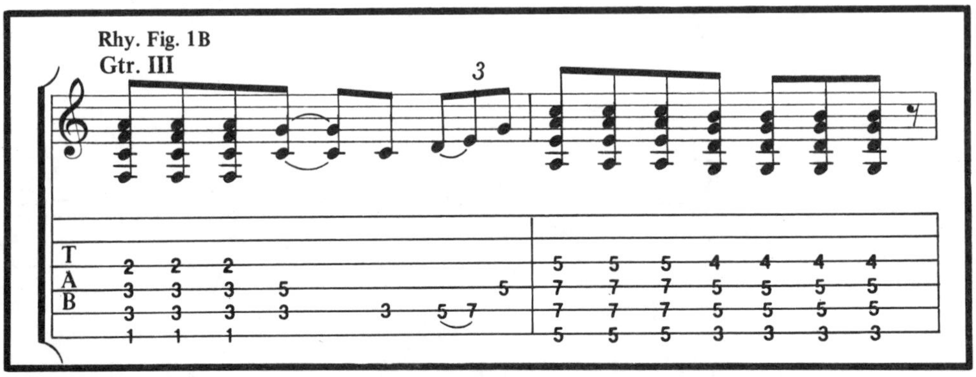
Rhy. Fig. 1B
Gtr. III

Guitar Solo: w/Rhy. Figs. 1 & 1A (Gtrs. 1 & 3)
Gtrs. I & III
G Gsus G Gsus G Gsus G Gsus G
F C Am G
*Gtr. II
hold
T A B
*slide guitar
(end solo)
Verse 4:
w/Rhy. Fig. 1
w/Rhy. Riff A
(8 times)
Well some say life will
beat you down, break your heart,
steal your crown.
Verse 5:
w/Rhy. Fig. 1A (4 times)
So I've start - ed out for
Ooh, ooh.
God knows where. I guess I'll know
Ooh, ooh.
when I get there. I'm
Ooh, ooh.
D.S. al Coda

Gtrs. I & III
Coda
Am G
G Gsus G Gsus G Gsus G Gsus G
T
A
B
(8) 3 5 7
F C Am G F C
Chorus:
w/Rhy. Figs 1 & 1B (12 times)
w/Rhy. Riff B (3 times)
w/Fill 1
Am G F C Am G
I'm learn - ing to fly
Learn - ing to fly.
but I
F C Am G F C
ain't got wings.
Com - ing down
Am G F C Am G
is the hard - est thing.
I'm
w/Fill 2
F C Am G F
learn - ing to fly
Learn - ing to fly.
a - round the clouds.
Fill 1
*Gtr. II
13 1
*w/slide
Fill 2
*Gtr. II
8 8 (8) (8) 0 0
*w/slide

Chorus 3:
Learning to fly,
Around the clouds.
What goes up,
Must come down.
(To Coda)

INTO THE GREAT WIDE OPEN

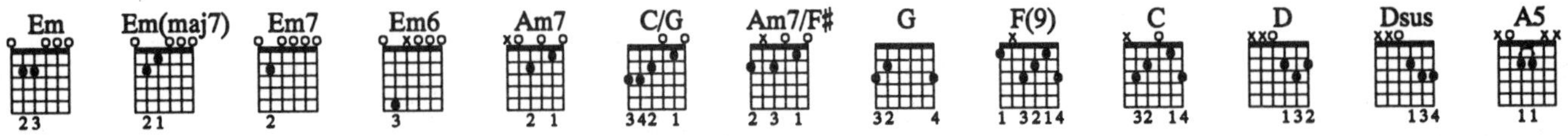

Words and Music by
TOM PETTY and JEFF LYNNE

Moderate rock ♩ **= 82**
Intro:

Gtr.1 w/Rhy. fig. 1
Em Em(maj7) Em7 Em6 Em Em(maj7)
They moved in - to a place they both could af - ford. He found a night - club he could
Gtr. 2
Rhy. fig. 2
(end Rhy. fig. 2)
hold
(Gtr. 1 cont. simile)
Em7 Em6 Am7 C/G Am7/F♯ C/G
work at the door. She had a gui - tar and she taught him some chords. The
hold
G F(9) C G C G
sky was the lim - it.
Chorus:
Rhy. fig. 3
(Gtr. 1 cont. simile)
C G D Dsus D Dsus G C D
In - to the great wide o - pen,
Rhy. fig. 3a
hold

G Em D Am G C D
un - der them skies __ of blue. Out in the great _ wide o - pen, a
hold
To Coda
(end Rhy. fig 3)
G F Em A5 G C G
reb - el with - out __ a clue. __
(end Rhy. fig 3a)
hold
Solo:
w/Rhy. fig. 1
w/Rhy. fig. 2 (2 times)
C G Em Em(maj7) Em7 Em6 Em Em(maj7)
Gtr. 3
hold
Verse 2:
w/Rhy. fig. 2 (2 times) (Gtr. 2)
end solo
w/Rhy. fig. 1 (Gtr.1)
Em7 Em6 Em Em(maj7) Em7 Em6 Em Em(maj7)
2. The pa-pers said Ed al-ways played from the heart. _ He got an a- gent and a
Gtr.3 (w/slide)

(Gtr. 1 cont. simile)
Em7 Em6 Am7 C/G Am7/F# C/G G F(9)
road-ie named Bart._ They made a re-cord and it went in the charts._ The sky was the
Gtr. 2
w/Rhy. fig. 1
w/Rhy. fig. 2 (2 times)
C G C G Em Em(maj7) Em7 Em6
li-mit. His leath-er jack-et had chains that would jin-gle.
Em Em(maj7) Em7 Em6 Am7/F# G Am7 C
They both met mov-ie stars, par-tied and min-gled. Their A and R man said, "I don't hear a sin-gle." The
D.S. al Coda
G F(9) C G C G C G D Dsus D Dsus
fu-ture was wide o-pen.

Coda
Chorus:
w/Rhy. figs. 3 & 3a (Gtrs. 1&2)
Em A5 G C D
In - to the great wide o - pen,
G Em D Am G C
un - der them skies of blue. In - to the great wide
D G F Em A5 G
o - pen, a reb - el with - out a clue.
C G C G

MARY JANE'S LAST DANCE

Words and Music by
TOM PETTY

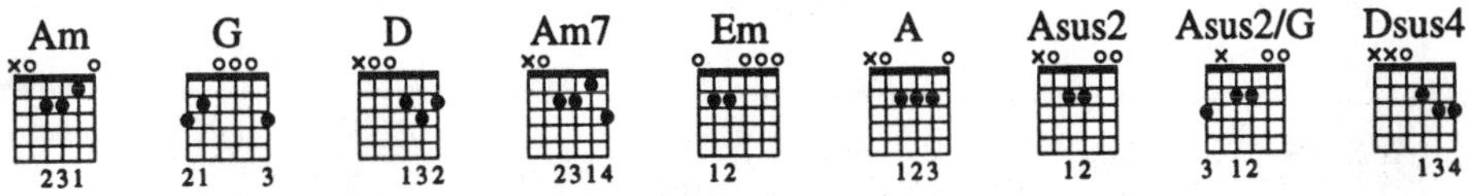

Gtrs.: Capo 1 (Song sounds 1/2 step higher than written)

Moderately ♩ = 88

Intro:

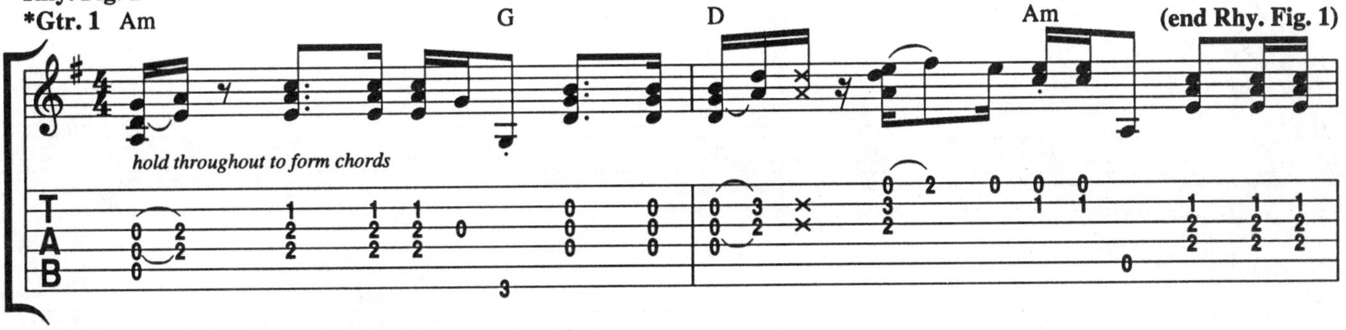

*Semi-distorted with a loose feel and partially muted strings.

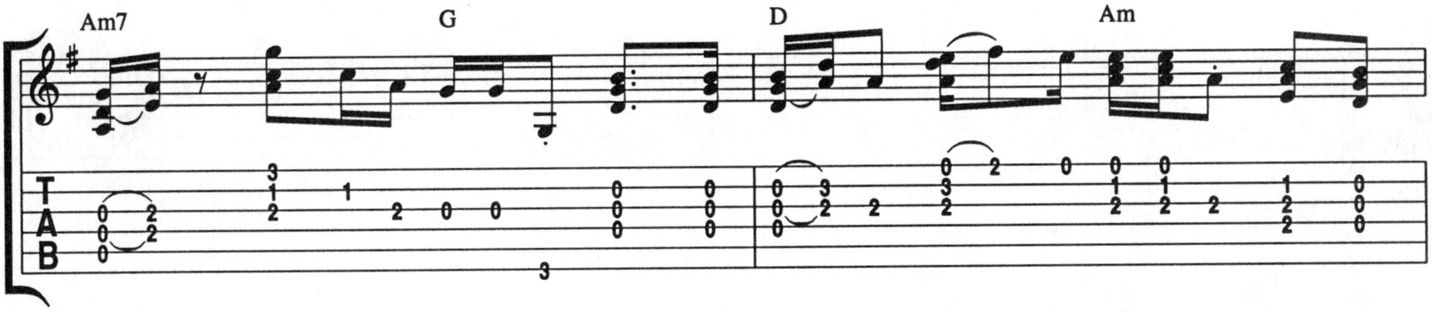

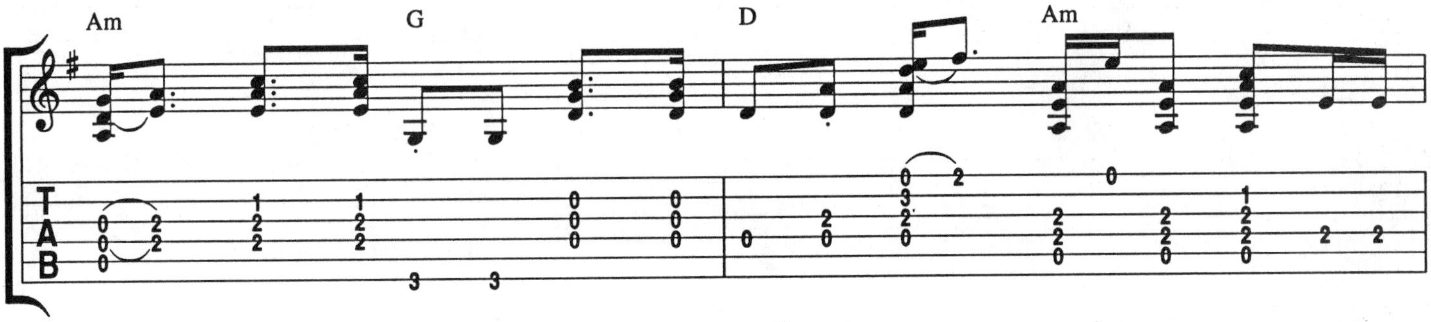

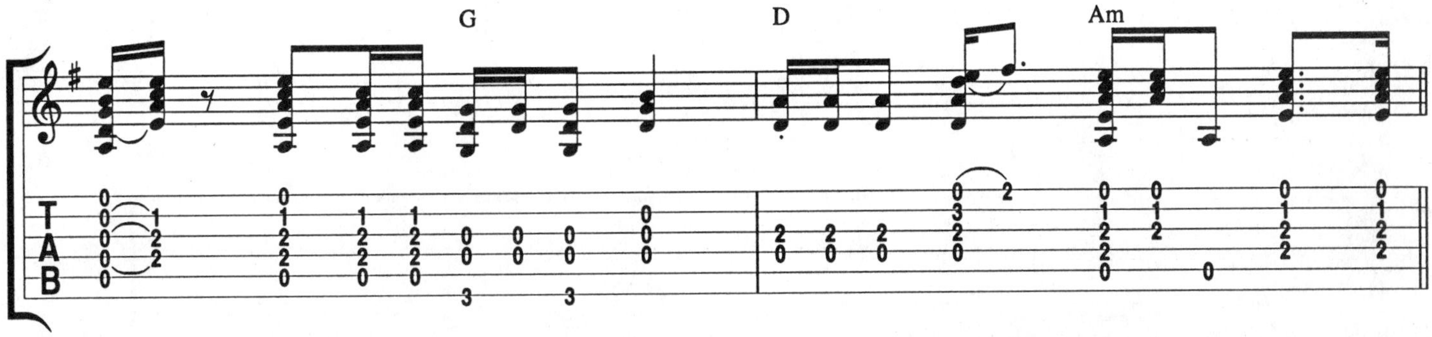

Verse 1:

Gtr. 1 *cont. simile*

G
D
Am
1. She grew up in a In - di - an - a town, had a good look-in' ma - ma who nev - er was a-round. But she

G D Am
grew up tall __ and she grew up right _ with them In - di - an - a boys on an In - di - an - a night.
Voc. Fig. 1
(end Voc. Fig. 1)
Am7 G D Am Am7 G D Am
Bkgd: Hoo.
Hoo.
2. Then she
Verses 2, 3 & 4:
Gtr. 1 cont. simile
G D Am
moved down here at the age of eight - een, she blew the boys a - way; was more _ than they'd seen.
3.4. See additional lyrics
*Gtr. 2
T
A
B
*partially muted strings
substitute w/Fill 1 (Gtr. 2, 2nd time)
G D Am
I was in - tro - duced and we both start - ed groov - in', she said I dig you ba - by but I got to keep mov - in'
Fill 1
Gtr. 2
hold

Am7
G
D
Am
on.
Keep mov-in' on.
Am7
G
D
Am
Chorus:
Em
Rhy. cont. simile
Last dance with Mar - y Jane,
one more time to kill the pain.
Asus2
A
hold
hold

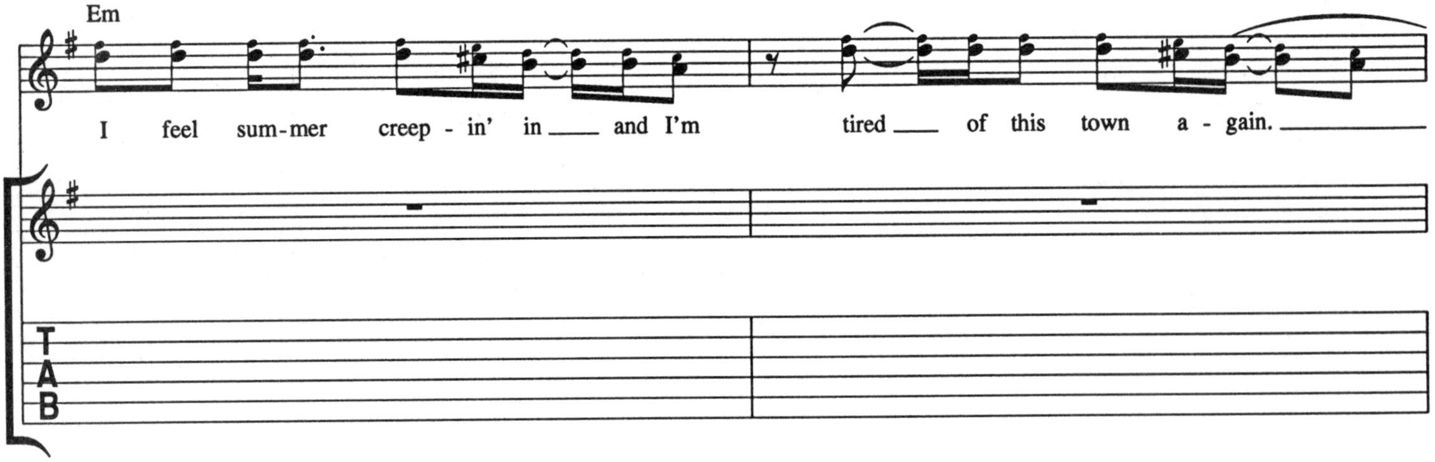
Em
I feel sum-mer creep - in' in ___ and I'm tired ___ of this town a - gain. ___
TAB

substitute w/Fill 2 (Gtr. 2, 3rd time)
To Coda
Asus2
Asus2/G
hold
hold
TAB

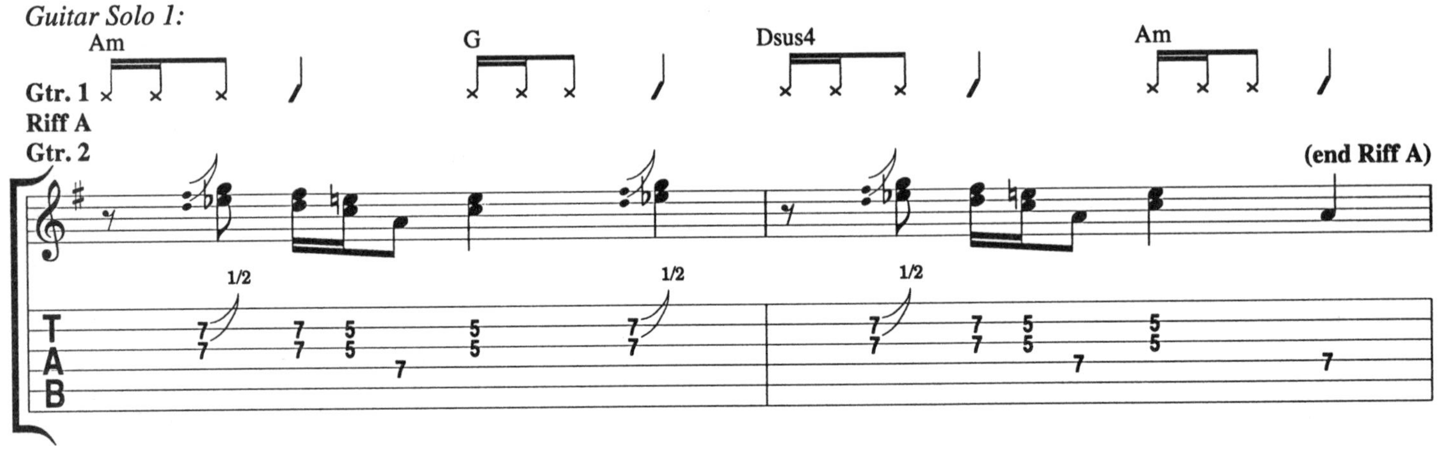
Guitar Solo 1:
Am
G
Dsus4
Am
Gtr. 1
Riff A
Gtr. 2
(end Riff A)
1/2
1/2
1/2
TAB

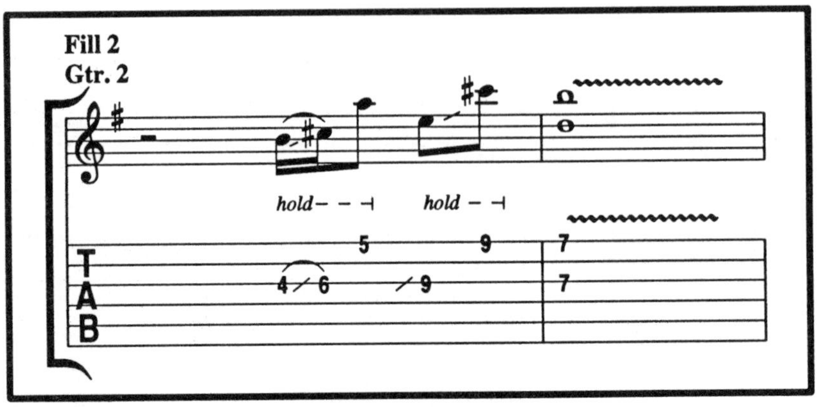
Fill 2
Gtr. 2
hold
hold
TAB

Gtr. 1 Cont. rhy. simile
G
Dsus4
Am
*Gtr. 3
*Heavy distortion
Gtr. 3
G
Dsus4
Am
hold
D.S. al Coda
G
Dsus4
Am
hold
Coda
Harmonica Solo:
w/Rhy. Fig. 1 (Gtr. 1)
w/Rhy. Fig. 1 (Gtr. 1), Riff A (Gtr. 2) & Voc. Fig. 1
Am
G
D
Am
G
D
Am
Guitar Solo 2:
w/Rhy. Fig. 1 (Gtr. 1) & Riff A (Gtr. 2)
Gtr. 3
G
D
Am
hold

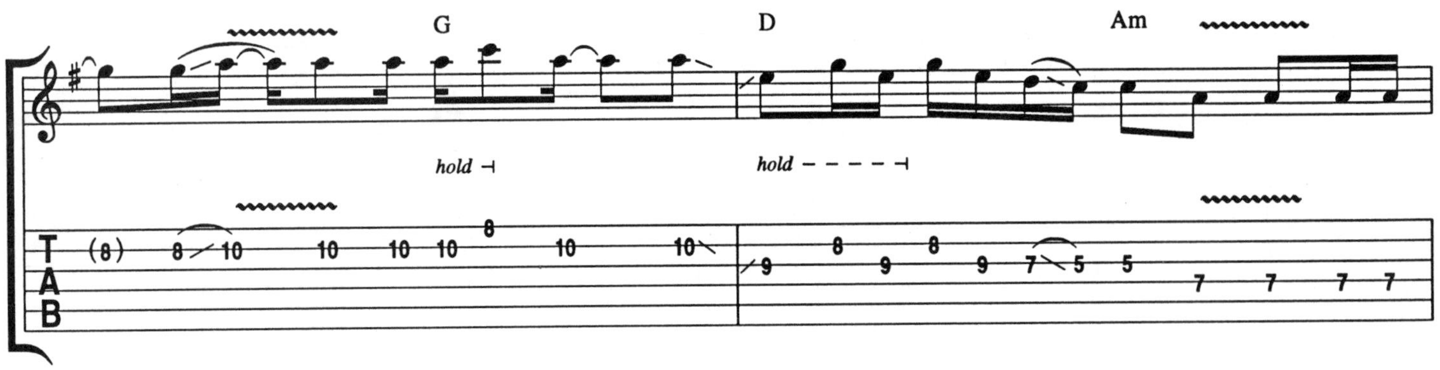

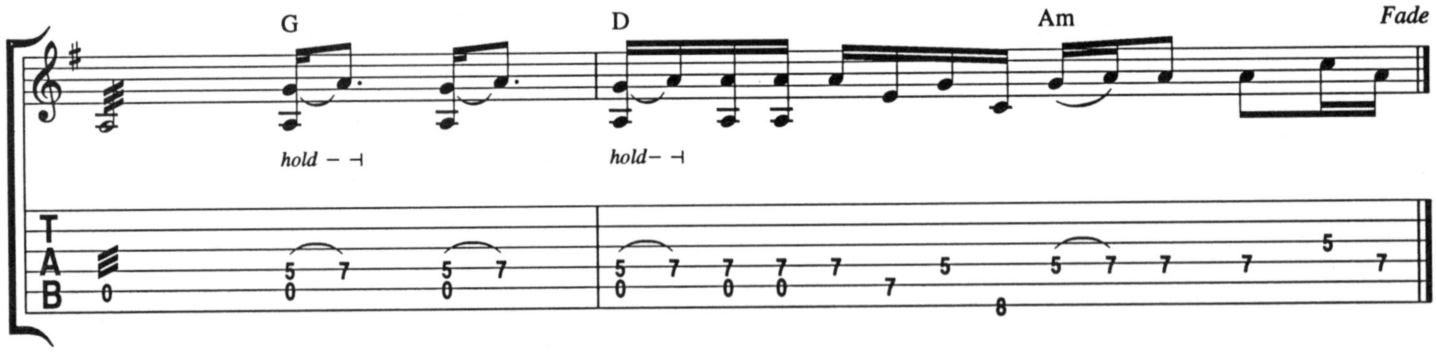

Verse 3:
Well I don't know but I been told, you never slow down, you never grow old.
I'm tired of screwin' up, tired of goin' down,
Tired of myself, tired of this town.
Oh my, my, oh hell yes - Honey put on that party dress.
Buy me a drink, sing me a song,
Take me as I come cause I can't stay long.
(To Chorus:)

Verse 4:
There's pigeons down on Market Square,
She's standing in her underwear.
Lookin' down from a hotel room,
Nightfall will be coming soon.
Oh my, my, oh hell yes, you got to put on that party dress.
It was too cold to cry, when I woke up alone.
I hit my last number, I walked to the road.
(To Chorus:)

SOMETHING IN THE AIR

Words and Music by
JOHN KEENE

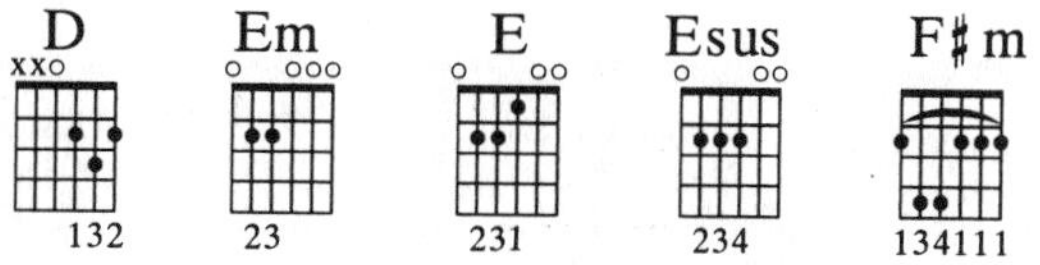

Em
rev - o - lu - tion's here, and you know it's right.
rev - o - lu - tion's here, and you know it's right.
hold
Pre-Chorus 1 & 2:
(D) (D/C) (D/B) (D/C) (D) (D/C) (D/B) (D/C)
And you know that it's right.
Gtr. 1
Gtr. 2
Em
We have got to get it to - geth - er, we have got to

1.
(D)
(D/C)
(D/B)
(D/C)
(D)
(D/C)
get it to-geth - er now.
hold
hold
(D/B)
(D/C)
2.
Bridge:
D7
now.
Gtr. 1
(hold)
Gtr. 2
(hold)
hold
hold
hold

C7
D7
(w/slide)
hold
C7
B♭7
A7
G7
A7
B7

Verse 3:
E Esus E Esus E
Gtr. 1
Call out the in - sti - ga - tor be - cause there's
Gtr. 2
(w/o slide)
hold
hold
hold
F♯m E
some - thing in the air.
We've got to get to - geth - er soon - er or lat -
hold
hold
hold
F♯m
er be - cause the rev - o - lu - tion's here, and you know it's right.

Pre-Chorus 3:
(E) (E/D) (E/C♯) (E/D) (E) (E/D)
And you know that it's
Gtr. 1
Gtr. 2
(E/C♯) (E/D)
Chorus 3:
F♯m
right.
We have got to get it to - geth - er,
hold
E
we have got to get it to - geth - er now.

GUITAR TAB GLOSSARY **

TABLATURE EXPLANATION

READING TABLATURE: Tablature illustrates the six strings of the guitar. Notes and chords are indicated by the placement of fret numbers on a given string(s).

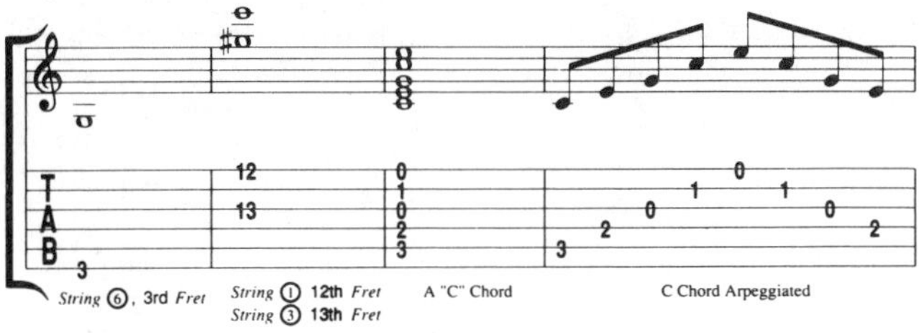

BENDING NOTES

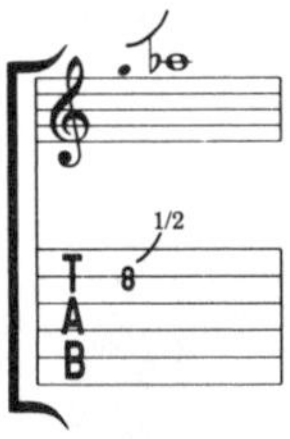

HALF STEP: Play the note and bend string one half step.*

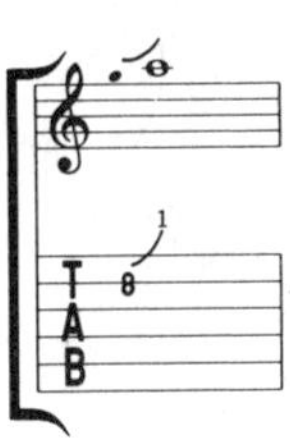

WHOLE STEP: Play the note and bend string one whole step.

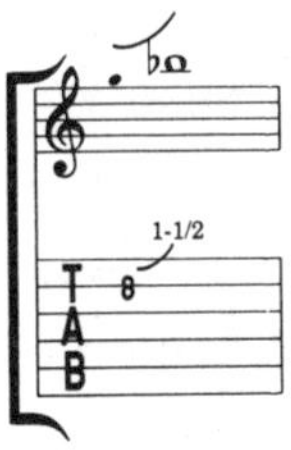

WHOLE STEP AND A HALF: Play the note and bend string a whole step and a half.

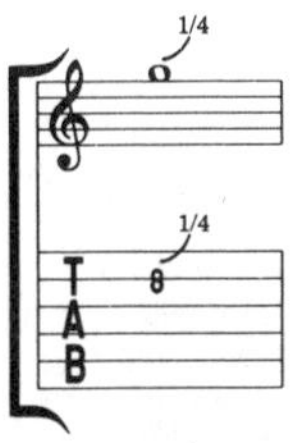

SLIGHT BEND (Microtone): Play the note and bend string slightly to the equivalent of half a fret.

*A half step is the smallest interval in Western music; it is equal to one fret. A whole step equals two frets.

PREBEND (Ghost Bend): Bend to the specified note, before the string is picked.

PREBEND AND RELEASE: Bend the string, play it, then release to the original note.

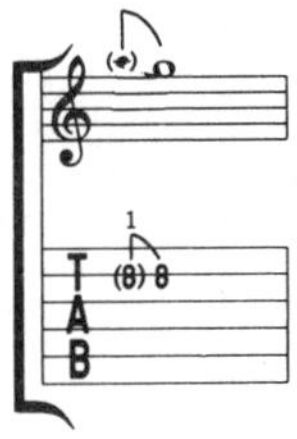

REVERSE BEND: Play the already-bent string, then immediately drop it down to the fretted note.

BEND AND RELEASE: Play the note and gradually bend to the next pitch, then release to the original note. Only the first note is attacked.

UNISON BEND: Play both notes and immediately bend the lower note to the same pitch as the higher note.

DOUBLE NOTE BEND: Play both notes and immediately bend both strings simultaneously.

BENDS INVOLVING MORE THAN ONE STRING: Play the note and bend string while playing an additional note (or notes) on another string(s). Upon release, relieve pressure from additional note(s), causing original note to sound alone.

BENDS INVOLVING STATIONARY NOTES: Play notes and bend lower pitch, then hold until release begins (indicated at the point where line becomes solid).

TREMOLO BAR

SPECIFIED INTERVAL: The pitch of a note or chord is lowered to a specified interval and then may or may not return to the original pitch. The activity of the tremolo bar is graphically represented by peaks and valleys.

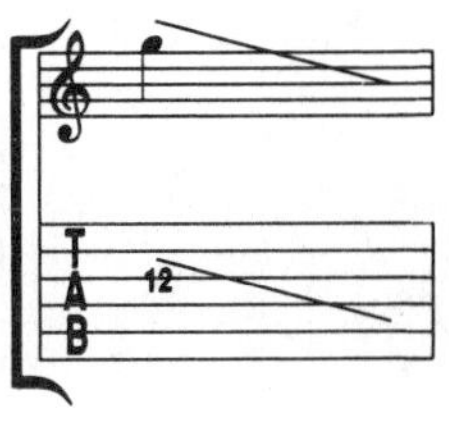

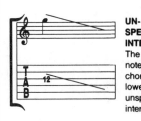

UN-SPECIFIED INTERVAL: The pitch of a note or a chord is lowered to an unspecified interval.

HARMONICS

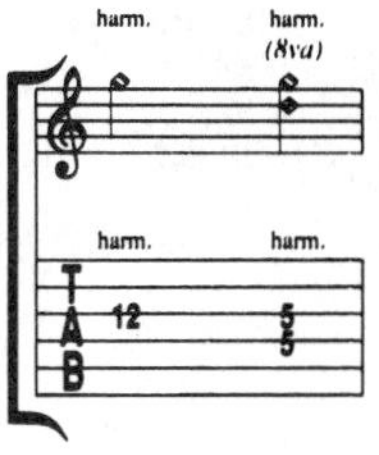

NATURAL HARMONIC: A finger of the fret hand lightly touches the note or notes indicated in the tab and is played by the pick hand.

ARTIFICIAL HARMONIC: The first tab number is fretted, then the pick hand produces the harmonic by using a finger to lightly touch the same string at the second tab number (in parenthesis) and is then picked by another finger.

ARTIFICIAL "PINCH" HARMONIC: A note is fretted as indicated by the tab, then the pick hand produces the harmonic by squeezing the pick firmly while using the tip of the index finger in the pick attack. If parenthesis are found around the fretted note, it does not sound. No parenthesis means both the fretted note and A.H. are heard simultaneously.

**By Kenn Chipkin and Aaron Stang

RHYTHM SLASHES

STRUM INDICATIONS: Strum with indicated rhythm. The chord voicings are found on the first page of the transcription underneath the song title.

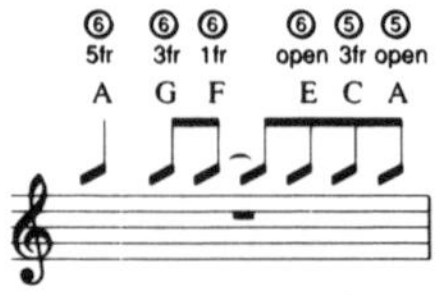

INDICATING SINGLE NOTES USING RHYTHM SLASHES: Very often single notes are incorporated into a rhythm part. The note name is indicated above the rhythm slash with a fret number and a string indication.

ARTICULATIONS

HAMMER ON: Play lower note, then "hammer on" to higher note with another finger. Only the first note is attacked.

LEFT HAND HAMMER: Hammer on the first note played on each string with the left hand.

PULL OFF: Play higher note, then "pull off" to lower note with another finger. Only the first note is attacked.

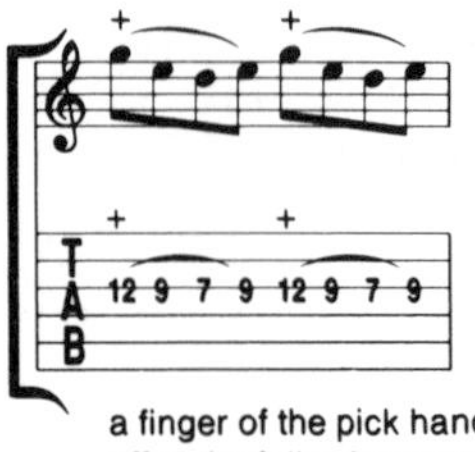

FRETBOARD TAPPING: "Tap" onto the note indicated by + with a finger of the pick hand, then pull off to the following note held by the fret hand.

TAP SLIDE: Same as fretboard tapping, but the tapped note is slid randomly up the fretboard, then pulled off to the following note.

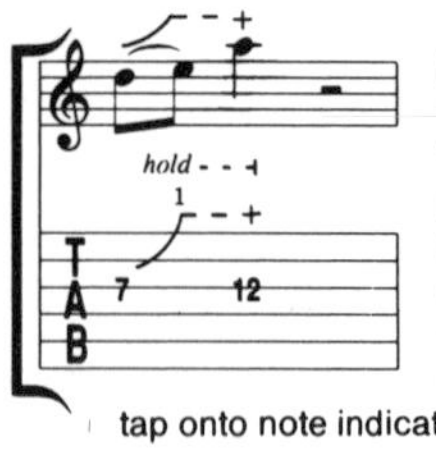

BEND AND TAP TECHNIQUE: Play note and bend to specified interval. While holding bend, tap onto note indicated.

LEGATO SLIDE: Play note and slide to the following note. (Only first note is attacked).

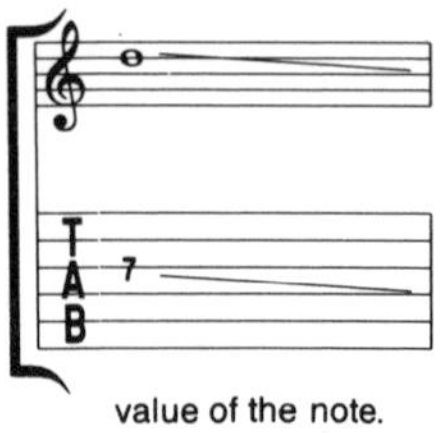

LONG GLISSANDO: Play note and slide in specified direction for the full value of the note.

SHORT GLISSANDO: Play note for its full value and slide in specified direction at the last possible moment.

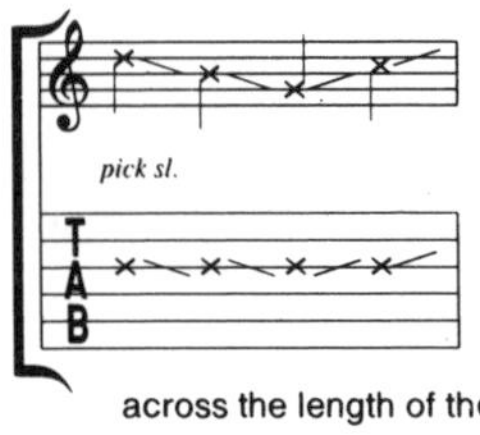

PICK SLIDE: Slide the edge of the pick in specified direction across the length of the string(s).

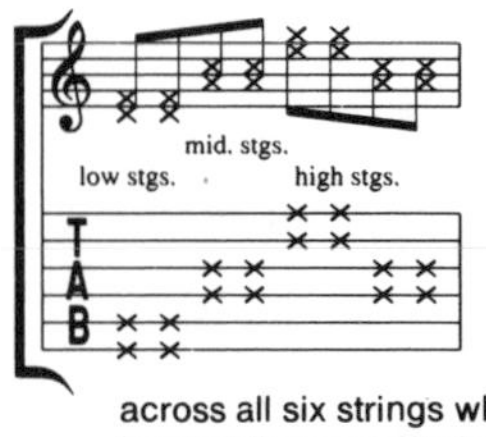

MUTED STRINGS: A percussive sound is made by laying the fret hand across all six strings while pick hand strikes specified area (low, mid, high strings).

PALM MUTE: The note or notes are muted by the palm of the pick hand by lightly touching the string(s) near the bridge.

TREMOLO PICKING: The note or notes are picked as fast as possible.

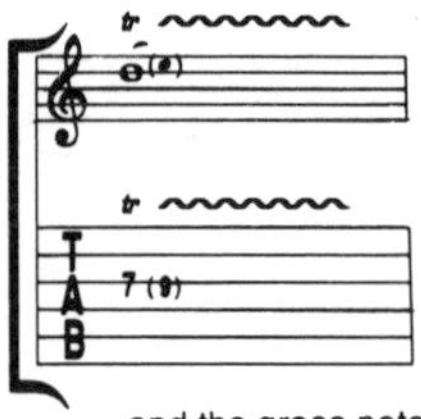

TRILL: Hammer on and pull off consecutively and as fast as possible between the original note and the grace note.

ACCENT: Notes or chords are to be played with added emphasis.

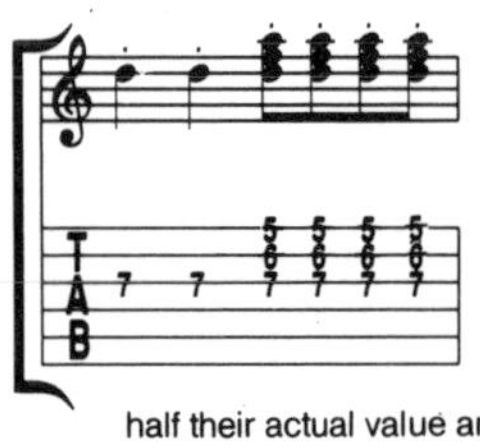

STACCATO (Detached Notes): Notes or chords are to be played roughly half their actual value and with separation.

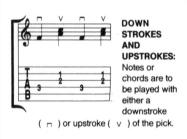

DOWN STROKES AND UPSTROKES: Notes or chords are to be played with either a downstroke (⊓) or upstroke (∨) of the pick.

VIBRATO: The pitch of a note is varied by a rapid shaking of the fret hand finger, wrist, and forearm.

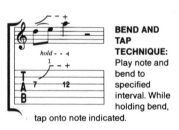

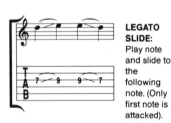

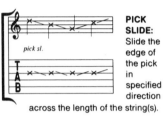

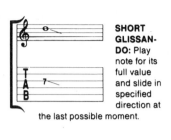

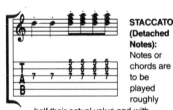